News Media

The Weak Slat Under
the Bed of Democracy

John Randolph Parker

ISBN: 1-4033-0965-5 (Paperback)
ISBN: 1-4033-0964-7 (e-book)

This book is printed on acid free paper.

1stBooks - rev. 06/19/02

"I'm Mad As Hell and I'm Not Going to Take It Anymore!"

From the film: *Network*

INTRODUCTION

Have you ever wondered why creative fields such as journalism, film, stage, television and advertising hand out so many prizes to their practitioners each year for "excellence?" Think about it: Do Ford, General Motors, Chrysler, Toyota and other auto makers gather together each year to award "Best Car in Sedan Class" or "Best Foreign Car With At Least Four Cylinders"? Not yet anyway. Have you ever heard of Pfizer or Warner-Lambert walking off to thunderous applause with a "Drug of the Year" award?

Several of the media's prize awarding ceremonies provide much of America with some of the most watched entertainment during the year. As winter fades into spring half the world lies in bed anxious to learn who will win an *Oscar* for best lighting in a movie about chain saws, or which mediocre musical will grab a *Tony* for choreography for more than one dancer, or who will win an *Emmy* for best acting in a situation comedy that is not half as funny as *Seinfeld*, or who will win an *Obie* for off-Broadway excellence (but not good enough, mind you, to make it to Broadway to compete for a *Tony*), or who will win a *Clio* for the most ridiculous—but funny, commercial shown during the Super Bowl. Lest we forget, we want to know who will win a *Pulitzer Prize* for being the best damned (and luckiest) newspaper or reporter or editorial writer in America or a *Peabody* for the best quasi-serious televised program or commentator of the year. The list seems endless. The main beneficiaries of this focus on giving awards happen to be a couple of the recipients and reporters of these events: newspapers, magazines and television, all of which make certain that the proceedings and award results receive maximum publicity which helps to bring in buckets full of advertising revenue.

A network willing to cough up a fortune to televise the Academy Awards stands to make more than a modest profit when its sales team fans out across the land touting the size of the expected viewing audience for that year's Oscars. Various newspapers and magazines will ballyhoo the Oscars as resembling the second coming, with lots of features on who is nominated and who can be expected to win. This will help boost circulation for a few days.

Publications fortunate enough to garner a Pulitzer for themselves or one or more of their writers will give the awards front page treatment. Runners-up or never-wases will report the news, but don't count on a headline larger than 12 point Bodoni. Joan Rivers has made a late career move of interviewing celebs about their fashion designer dresses pre, during and post Academy Awards. She's like that energized bunny.

This is all part of providing NEWS, but is actually a severe case of shameful narcissism. The awards fall into the same category as media-sponsored polls, polls which, by the way, helped to keep a disgraced president in office. This is how it works: The network or newspaper or magazine conducts a poll. The network or newspaper or magazine or any combination thereof, then reports the results of that poll. This provides the media involved with a "news" story. The steady increase in media polling over the years has provided media outlets with seemingly exciting news when there really isn't much exciting news to be had. It helps to fill time and space. Poll reporting has become as regular as weather reporting by television and radio and astrology columns in the print media.

Don't forget that the Associated Press, United Press International, Reuters and other news gathering and disseminating services were created to provide news fodder for publications and broadcast media which, alone, would be incapable of providing enough staff created stories to fill a newspaper bloated with the necessary portion of advertising lineage. For some publications with modest budgets and, therefore, limited staffs, wire service stories are absolutely necessary if they are to continue in business. Without this outside help, many couldn't fill their products with enough material to complement the pages of advertising lineage.

More polling there will be, even though there is evidence that the public is growing increasingly cranky about being polled. Recent reports on the subject indicate that about half of those folk called by pollsters hang up on the caller. This should come as no surprise. It is difficult to find anyone who has anything positive to say about telemarketing representatives who call when a family has just sat down to dinner, or made a rendezvous with the bathroom or even when the light has just been turned off in preparation for a good night's sleep. Yet polling goes on and will continue as long as *someone* can be found who won't hang up. Many political observers have agreed that Bill Clinton's high polling favorability numbers saved him from being forced to resign. During the Lewinski matter many persons noted that the polling being reported was somehow tainted. It wasn't unusual to hear complaints about polling at social gatherings or on the omni-present political talk shows. As recently as late November 1999, the New York Times carried a long article on Sunday that finally recognized what average citizens had been talking about for months. The article stated that pollsters were being hung up on by the persons they called. The reason was obvious: People have grown tired of telemarketing calls and often think a pollster's call is actually someone trying to sell something. The Times article revealed that poll takers are very much aware of the growing problem of finding enough people who don't slam down the phone. Yet, polling continues apace. It's the ability to report a poll's findings that makes news for print and broadcast, not the validity of the poll itself.

We have been told for years that most people receive almost all of their news via television. As a result, newspapers have been fighting a losing battle to retain circulation. An editor of the prestigious *Chicago Tribune* confessed on one of those omni-present media panel programs on cable television that his paper puts damned near anything on the front page in an effort to woo people to buy the paper and read what is inside. *Hype* seems to be an adequate operative word for this practice. This practice rivals those signs in gift shops that line New York streets that shout, "Going Out of Business. Prices Slashed! Everything Must Go!" Many of these stores have had such signs in their windows for several years. They, like the newspapers that hype their front page news stories and television stations that get downright giddy about non-news stories, are simply fighting for survival.

There is increasing evidence that there is less to news than meets the eye. There is also increasing evidence that the narcissistic news media, while devoting much of its time to self back patting, is the target of almost unending criticism, much of it from within their own tent.

Sydney Schanberg is a Pulitzer Prize winner for his work in Cambodia. He stirred things up at the *New York Times* and *Newsday* before landing with an online news service which covers crime and the justice system. In an Outlook piece in the Washington Post he laid into his profession of journalism.

"It's no secret that journalism in America," he wrote, "has become more slipshod and reckless, at times promiscuous—and as a result less credible."

Schanberg accused editors and owners and some top journalists of rationalizing that the speed of cyberspace and all-news cable outlets are the "competitive devils" that cause this lessening of gravity.

"The new mantras of editors and media proprietors," he concluded, "seems to be: 'We have no choice but to cut corners if we are to survive'."

Schanberg is no shrinking violet. He's never been reluctant to toss a bit of unpleasantness into a punch bowl. He called for newspapers to establish a "press beat." He is not hopeful. He declared that print media don't even try to cover themselves. Of the some 1,500 papers in the country, Schanberg noted that there are only a handful that have a reporter covering the press full time. Not surprisingly, he observed that most of this reporting is "timid and superficial."

I

PHONINESS SYNDROME

Poor Jessica Savich. I established the *Jessica Savich Award* long before she was tragically killed in a bizarre automobile accident that was somewhat reminiscent of what happened at Chappaquiddick. Following a dinner with her boy friend, the car in which they were riding went off a bridge and plunged them to their death in the water below.

Savich was an attractive blond who had established herself as an anchorperson on various local and network stations. There have been reports that she had drug and emotional problems.

The *Jessica Savich Award* was created to call attention to the tendency of television talking heads to attempt to fool viewers by pretending to look downward occasionally, while they are delivering

1

to the public the very latest in exciting, now-don't- miss-this news. This is to give the impression that they are not reading from a Teleprompter, but are actually reading from notes or a script that is before them on the desk, notes that viewers are to believe they painstakingly wrote themselves. The downward glance takes but an instant, giving rise to speculation that all talking heads are magna cum laude graduates of the Evelyn Wood speed reading course.

Ms. Savich did the following to prompt establishment of the award: Near the very end of one of her news broadcasts, she looked downward as if to check her "notes." She then looked up and said, "This is Jessica Savich for ABC News." Apparently, the poor woman had to look at her "notes" to recall her own name! I have seen this happen many, many times.

ABC's Diane Sawyer happens to be a totally inept practitioner of the "nod and look up" technique. She barely takes time to look downward, opting, instead, to start a downward gaze, but suddenly looking up in one fluid motion. It's the same maneuver as an unfortunate who tends to nod off during a boring speech only to rally just before chin meets chest.

It has always been thus. NBC's Tom Brokaw does it, as do ABC's Peter Jennings and CBS's Dan Rather. Heck, even Walter Cronkite, "the most trusted man in America" while at CBS did it. Local newscasters do it as well, only not as effectively as the mega-buck network anchors which, one assumes, is one of the reasons they are not at the network level.

Check it out. The next time you watch a newscast, note how many times the person reading from a Teleprompter looks down to check his or her "notes." Moreover, try to detect what has come to be known as the *Saint Vitas Dance* method of reading the news. This occurs when the person reading the news moves his or her head to and fro and up and down so the viewer will be unable to focus on the reader's eyes moving laterally, giving away the obvious that what is said is actually being read. Some talking heads are so hyper that they give viewers the impression that they could possibly faint from dizziness because of the sudden twists and turns. Check out Mike Wallace during one of his *60 Minutes* segments. Wallace has one of the busiest faces on television. He slyly adds a *wince* now and then to steer viewers away from any side-to-side eye movement that would be a dead giveaway that he is totally reliant on the Teleprompter.

In this same category of trying to fool the public, have you ever wondered what it is exactly that anchors do with all of those papers they keep in front of them while reading from the Teleprompter? One assumes that that's what they are looking at from time to time. It is at the end of a program that the stack of papers really comes into play. When the person or persons give their sign off, and there is a second or two to fill before the camera leaves them, they are always busily reshuffling those papers to beat the band. Some anchors, especially local talking heads, not only shuffle those papers but occasionally pound them with their fists or open palms for emphasis. They presumably do this until the camera is no longer on them to give themselves something to do that looks vaguely like work. When the camera no longer shows them, those papers usually wind up in a waste basket, according to a television executive I interviewed for this book. One of life's genuine entertainments, by the way, occurs when the camera takes longer than it should to sign off. The talking heads look so darn uncomfortable when this happens.

Let's say an anchor excitedly tells viewers that, "We will now go to Harriet Higsby, live, at the scene where the unfortunate motorist experienced a flat tire." The anchor describes this in somewhat breathless tones and turns slightly to fix his or her gaze on the studio monitor so as not to miss any of the exciting story that is coming to everyone "live." Are we to believe the anchor actually sits at the desk gazing intently at the monitor while the live report is being given. More likely, he or she is running to the bathroom or chatting with colleagues while the camera is off them while Ms. Higsby is at the scene bringing us that exciting story to us "Live!"

Jessica, we hardly knew ye.

"Gone are the days that we had to wait for Dan Rather to put on his makeup to read us the evening news. Gone is the time when a few newspaper and magazine editors controlled the flow and owned the headlines."

Matt Drudge
The Drudge Report

II

RATING THE ANCHORS

It hasn't been that long ago that the network anchors were all men who obviously had writing ability and some experience as news reporters. Nowadays many anchors are obviously chosen because of their blondness or beauty or ability to wear a suit and tie that do not clash. Apparently writing is a talent that is not at all necessary to become a television talking head. If you doubt this, rush to any event at which a highly paid, experienced TV journalist is a guest speaker and you will hear him say the same thing.

In television's infancy, Edward R. Murrow led CBS News to the head of the class. Murrow gave the news through clouds of cigarette smoke that would send him to an early grave. He surrounded himself with men who had paid their dues during World War II, reporting the war "from the front." They were all believable because of their obvious backgrounds as serious reporters, although Murrow ironically had virtually no reporting background before he grabbed the brass ring from CBS.

Then came a network decision to pair two newscasters, Chet Huntley and David Brinkley. They stole the show from CBS at political conventions which, at that time, were interesting and fun to watch for educational and informational reasons as well as the entertainment value. Huntley and Brinkley continued their convention momentum and made, "Good night Chet...Good night David," the words much of America heard at the end of their favorite newscast. Cigarette (Brinkley) and pipe (Huntley) smoke could be seen from time to time during the news broadcast. This was, of course, long before entire buildings became non-smoking zones.

Once CBS got over the Huntley and Brinkley shock, that network installed Walter Cronkite as its anchor and he did battle with NBC's dynamic duo for many years. Cronkite retired, Huntley died and Brinkley eventually stepped aside to do other things. Then came a period of uncertainty among the networks as to whom to install in the all-important anchor chairs.

Roger Mudd almost single handedly wrecked Teddy Kennedy's final presidential express by showing the Massachusetts legislator to be less than erudite during a pivotal television interview. Mudd was hot stuff at CBS for awhile but not for long. He just didn't seem to fit CBS's idea of a replacement for Cronkite. Finally, CBS decided to install Dan Rather as the single anchor to succeed Cronkite in what had become the most prestigious of the three networks anchor chairs. Mudd wound up at PBS, giving occasional political commentary and later did the same thing for The History Channel.

It has been many years that Rather has been bringing a portion of America the news, compliments of CBS. Strangely, he still seems to be trying to find his niche. He began by trying a Jimmy Carter-esque approach by wearing a sweater during his broadcast. That sartorial gesture was supposed to give him a warm and cuddly look, a la Cronkite. This didn't work, so he went back to wearing a suit. During promos that appear before his broadcast and during which he tells America what stories he is working on, he always appears in shirt sleeves and the obligatory Murrow-esque suspenders. Ostensibly this gives the appearance that he actually works to earn his multi-million dollar salary.

For the longest time, Rather appeared to be downright catatonic. At the close of his newscast each night he could be seen sitting in his anchor chair following his sign off, doing absolutely nothing. He just sat there! He talked with no one and stared straight ahead until the camera did a fade out. One wonders how he survived this period of truly embarrassing behavior—on camera! This highest paid anchor of them all also has a weird habit of winking at the audience. He actually winks from time to time, one assumes to emphasize a point he is making rather maladroitly. In his latest foray into trying to be "normal" he stopped dying his hair and as this is written shows up five nights a week in a virtual crew cut and a lot of gray, as if he is trying to look like Clint Eastwood as a Marine sergeant. As if to keep pace with Brokaw and Jennings who have produced best selling books about World War II and the 20th Century, Rather produced a book on outstanding people. Writing books seems to give these guys legitimacy, or at least they think so. How can they be empty suits or talking heads if they write (or have written for them) BOOKS!

Tom Brokaw and Peter Jennings have kept NBC and ABC ahead of Rather most of the time. First NBC and then ABC led the threesome. Brokaw is an example of how someone who doesn't fit the image of an anchor can become an anchor and stay there for years. Whatever his journalistic background, (he began and has remained in broadcast) viewers have never been made privy to it. He's just there. He is well dressed which is his strong suit because when he speaks, he occasionally gives the impression of having marbles in his mouth. He actually slurs certain words. (Apparently he has a problem with the letter "L".) He has explained that he does this when he is overly tired. His diction or lack thereof reminds one of the hilarious Peter Brook-Dudley Moore routine during which a one-legged man (Moore) shows up to audition for the part of Tarzan. Despite Brokaw's often satirized speaking deficiency, he remains at his post, anchoring NBC's nightly news, pulling down a salary to kill for. Really, who would hire a person who slurs words to be a network anchor?

Peter Jennings is every college dropout's dream because he never even went to college. Besides that, he was born and raised Canadian! (Only in America.)

Of the three anchors, he is by far the most articulate. He has a trenchcoat that he wears for live "remotes," that sets him apart from Brokaw and Rather, although the trenchcoat that Rather breaks out for remote assignments seems much older and threadbare. Jennings can do the look-down-look up routine better than his two counterparts at NBC and CBS. Comparatively speaking, he is smooth as silk. When ABC News slipped out of first place for a while, the network worked overtime to cauterize the leakage of rating points. Don't forget that just about every television news person admits that TV news is about ratings points much more than news.

Eventually, Jennings could be seen surrounded by the largest assembly of staff ever seen on a television screen. While he read from the Teleprompter the aides sat and busied themselves at their computers to give Jennings the very latest bulletins as they came in from around the world. Not surprisingly, the staffers work ended at the very instant Jennings called it quits for the day. As this is written Jennings can be seen walking around the set from time to time. Once, he actually looked as if he were heading to the loo just before a commercial break. Moving Jennings around the set was obviously one of ABC's answers to the declining ratings. It doesn't have anything to do with news; after all, TV is an entertainment business. Brokaw took to moving around his set as well to show Jennings that two could play that game. In fact, most anchors these days roam around the set as if they are trying to sneak up on some hapless cameraman to play "gotcha."

Americans have been receiving their nighty dole of news from Rather, Brokaw and Jennings for many years. They have stayed the course. It can only be assumed that their longevity has ruined the chances of many anchor wannabes who have waited in the network wings so long that their time for succession has come and gone. It is interesting to note which non-anchors who have been around for many years have resorted to hair dye to keep them current. One imagines they dye their hair not so much to fool the viewing public as to fool the network bosses who might have occasion to say, "You know, ol' Charlie is getting a little long in the tooth, wouldn't you say."

III

REPORTING ON REPORTERS

Just what is it that reporters do? We see them on television and we read their work in newspapers. But, really, how does a reporter go about gathering the news he or she reports. First, it is helpful to define what a reporter is. A reporter is not Barbara Walters or Diane Sawyer, or many of the anchors who appear on local news programs. A good example of the quality of reporters for local television stations was given when there was a fire some years ago in the press room of the *New York Daily News*. This could have been a big story, even in New York. Fortunately the fire was quickly extinguished, but for a short while there was quite a bit of frenzied activity in the art deco building on East 42nd Street. The word went out to news outlets throughout the city: "Fire in the headquarters of the nation's largest (at that time) newspaper!" In the midst of the flurry of activity to extinguish the blaze, a female reporter about 21 years old and her camera crew entered the *News* building. The "reporter" led the way and looked somewhat, shall we say, excited. This reporter, in charge of getting the story for her TV station, ran up to a non-*News* employee who was leaving the building to go home and shouted, "Show me someone important!" Obviously there would be no *Pulitzer* on her mantel any time soon.

That reporter would later appear on a news program and give the public her report on the fire at the *News*. She would appear to be relatively professional and competent. That appearance would be totally deceptive.

Ask yourself the following: If a television reporter appears on the screen once a day to give a 60- second report and that's all you see of him or her that day, how much actual work could have been done? Or if you read a rather dull newspaper story about a hearing at City Hall, have you ever wondered what else the reporter did that day to fill the eight hours for which he or she is paid?

If you happen to work for a company that closely supervises you during much of your eight-hour stint each day, you will be seriously envious of a reporter's workday. Visit any newspaper and examine the activity in the news room. You will probably see numerous college educated journalists sitting around doing a little bit of nothing for long periods of time. You will witness a man or woman writing a story, perhaps, of a high school remodeling program. The reporter will be talking on the telephone to a school spokesperson, tapping computer keys all the while. The reporter will look rather bored, because this story is not exactly potential for a promotion or raise. When not tapping those computer keys, the reporter will more than likely chat with a fellow reporter who is also without an exciting story to write.

Years ago reporters in a news room (many of whom never attended college) would discuss the finer points of placing bets with their bookies, or discussing local sports activity. The word, *fuck* in all its conjugations, could be heard with some frequency, unlike today when most reporters seem to be college educated and are relatively straight arrows, who almost certainly don't keep a bottle of blended whiskey in their desk drawer.

Let's take an imaginary journey to examine a newspaper reporter's typical work day:

. Show up at XYZ, Inc., to cover the dedication of a new wing that will house additional warehousing capability, important to the corporation and to its employees and relatives of those employees.

. Hang out. Chat with XYZ officers and employees, asking them questions, the answers to which can be used in the exciting news story to be written later.

. The company's CEO is a half hour late, so there is lots of just hanging around. By this time the reporter has run out of questions to ask.

. Go across the street and get a cup of coffee and a bagel with butter to go.

. Take a few notes of what the CEO says at the dedication once he shows up.

. Take cab back to newspaper. Fill out reimbursement form.

. Write story about that morning's experience. Try to make it sound exciting and important.

. Sit around and wait for another exciting assignment from an editor. Chat with fellow reporters who also are experiencing down time.

. The next assignment is to telephone another company officer and get about four column inches on the rumor that the company plans to move its headquarters out of town. Talk with a total stranger and type a four column inch story about why the rumor is said to be unfounded.

. Chat with other reporters for a while.

. Go home.

Next, let's explore a television reporter's work day:

. Leave home and go to station.

. Get assignment to take cameraman to City Hall to cover a report by the Finance Committee that may or may not increase income taxes.

. Go to City Hall and hang out with cameraman for an hour waiting for the committee to complete its work. Chat with other reporters.

. When committee members leave the committee room, rush up and ask whether taxes will or will not go up. When committee members leave, take an hour or so perfecting your report that the cameraman will record for use during the evening news show.

. Go back to station and await another exciting assignment.

. There is no additional assignment. Go home.

It is obvious that most reporters (there are some exceptions) are over paid for the amount of work they do. During the "old days" when John Kennedy was President and before it was not unusual to see highly regarded reporters who were assigned to cover Capitol Hill, playing cards during the rather lengthy periods when there was nothing happening on the House or Senate floor. Some were curled up on a bench, enjoying a nap. The next time you show up for work, try suggesting a game of "Hearts" or a refreshing nap with your co-workers and good luck at the Unemployment Office.

IV

IS THERE A LIBERAL BIAS?

Callers to C-Span and Larry King regularly accuse the media of being "soft" on liberal politicians. With some frequency during the many months before President Clinton confessed that he lied to the American public, many callers said things like, "Hey, if this had been Nixon, his ass would have been grass," or "If this has been a Republican, the media would have jumped on him like nobody's business."

There is some truth to this.

For instance:

Judge Robert Bork said on Ben Wattenberg's interview program that, "(The Clintons) are obviously guilty of obstruction of justice on

Travelgate, Filegate and the aftermath of the Vince Foster suicide." (Direct quote.)

This occurred long before Monica Lewinski got a rise out of the President. Bork was a professor of both Clintons when they were at Yale Law School. One would think that some newspaper or television reporter would have considered this a fairly juicy news story, with a headline that read, **"Former Law Professor Claims Clintons Guilty of Obstruction of Justice."**

There was nary a word of reportage of Bork's comment to be found in the print or broadcast media.

Chris Matthews was rewarded with another half hour for his "Hardball" program to stretch itself on CNBC. Night after night, Matthews hammered Clinton once the Lewinski story broke. A Democrat who worked for Tip O'Neal and Jimmy Carter, Matthews took umbrage over Clinton's loose grip on the truth. One evening he had the omnipresent Gennifer Flowers as a guest—for the entire hour. He and she agreed that Clinton also committed perjury when he testified under oath that he had had sex with Ms. Flowers, "Once." She allowed on national television for the umpteenth time that they had sex over a 12 year period. Again, it seems that a vigilant media would have come up with a headline something like: **GENNIFER FLOWERS AND CHRIS MATTHEWS AGREE: CLINTON COMMITTED PERJURY: AGAIN!**

Not a word was printed or spoken about this comment that had all the earmarks of a solid news story. Numerous other ladies claimed to have had affairs with the President, but these allegations failed to make the front page, or if reported at all, never achieved a headline set in anything above 18 point type.

The media's tendency to report trivial matters as lead stories was demonstrated once again in a column by Clinton's former factotum, Dick Morris. Morris wrote the following in the *New York Post* during Ms. Clinton's "listening" campaign to decide whether she should run for the U.S. Senate in New York:

"As she asked Rep. Nita Lowey to pull out, she promised that she would jump in during the fall. Now, during an upstate tour last week, she suddenly delays a decision until "sometime next year." While her flip-flop passed without journalistic or political comment, it deserves closer scrutiny."

Again, a seemingly significant news story passed without journalistic comment. In the spring of 2001, there was a flurry of news stories dealing with former U.S. Senator Robert Kerrey (D.,NEB.) and an alleged incident that occurred in Vietnam. The words, "war crime" actually surfaced as the story unfolded. It was somewhat embarrassing that much of the reporting was done by writers who never got close to Vietnam during the war. Andrew Sullivan, columnist for The New Republic, chimed in with some thoughts on the matter, a few of which called for a tribunal to decide whether Kerrey did, indeed, order the slaughter of civilian adults and children. He noted that Newsweek had "spiked" the story years before, not unlike its earlier handling of the Monica Lewinski/Bill Clinton matter.

In a column, Sullivan wrote: "Simple Question: Do you think if any evidence had emerged of, say, Oliver North's possible war crimes in Vietnam in identical terms—that Newsweek would have spiked the story?" Is there a liberal bias in the media. There certainly seems to be.

Creator of "60 Minutes", Don Hewitt, has written a book and has bounced around to just about television program known to man to plug his work. "Tell Me A Story," is the title and Hewitt has been raising eyebrows all over the lot as he shows up to help sell a few extra hundred thousand copies. Pre Book, as the saying is, I would have laid big money that Hewitt is as liberal as a Liberal can get. Hell, the show was the ultimate springboard for Bill and Hillary to move into 1600 Pennsylvania Avenue. But wait! During his countless interviews, Hewitt has claimed that he voted for Reagan, Bush, Sr., Bush, Jr., Lazio (take that Hillary!) and maintains those are his bona fides for being, well, if not a conservative, at least a moderate. He has told the world that he and everyone at "60 Minutes" knew Slick Willy and Hillary were lying during that famous interview.

Probably the most startling revelation from this world famous CBS producer, is that he believes that, eventually, the three big networks will throw in the towel and decide to pool what they've got into one entity. He maintains that networks give their affiliates all the news all day anyway and that the affiliates will decide in the end that they don't even need the "Evening News" because they've been reporting what Dan, Tom, and Peter will report all during the day.

Hewitt seems to be making eminent sense, so don't be surprised by anything that might transpire among the networks in the fairly near future.

V

LIARS, LIARS, PANTS ON FIRE!

A rhetorical proposal if you will: Let's say one of the networks comes on the air for the "Evening News" with the usual musical fanfare as the anchorperson breathlessly ticks off the program menu for that evening. He (or she) tells us that there will be a report on: A massive flood in the Ohio River basin; the signing of a left handed catcher by the New York Yankees; a new medicine that relieves itching from a dry scalp; and an interview with Donnie and Marie Osmond, done in the nude on a beach in Santa Monica. Which report would you be most interested in seeing? Almost certainly, you would be most anxious to check out that story on the Osmonds. Which subject do you believe will be the very last to be aired?

As we said, the question was rhetorical. There is absolutely no doubt that the Osmond interview would be dead last that evening. But, during the 22 minutes of fantastic "news" coming our way on the network, there would be incessant reminders, telling us that the Osmond interview was "coming up." This deception, of course, is supposed to lead us to believe that we will see this unusual event right after the umpteenth commercial message that contributes to the eight minutes of revenue gathering each half hour of "news."

The positioning of the juiciest story at the end of the program is not new. It has been the formula for years. The viewer wants to check out the Osmonds and go out and get some overdue gardening done. The network or local station manager knows this and keeps the prospective gardener in front of the TV set watching newsless news instead of outside in the fresh air by teasing him or her with the false likelihood that the bare Osmonds are next up.

Again, televised news programs, local or national, contain little news. Ask yourself when was the last time you watched Messrs. Rather, Jennings or Brokaw in action and found yourself saying, "Hey, I didn't know that!" or "Wow, how about that!" Let's face it: there simply isn't much real news. These days, news programs give a brief serving of news and, then, segue to magazine-type features.

It has long been a theory of mine that the only way we are going to save this republic of ours from cultural leprosy is to abolish daily news. Seriously! There just would not be daily newspapers or daily TV news programs. Maybe twice a week, but preferably once a week.

This would do away with the need to have the drum roll and images floating across the screen of well dressed, shirt sleeved news persons gathering news. There would be little or no need to hype stories of no real news value. This would remove the need for the news anchors (especially the local variety) to gush about non-stories. They would no longer be forced to impress the audience with the freshness of the non-fresh story by sounding excited about, well, nothing. On many local news shows the lead story every night seems to be a house fire somewhere in the city or state, or a robbery. Sometimes there are fatalities, most times, there are not. Just another house fire, just another robbery. There is always a report from the scene of the fire that comes to us "Live!" Often the local station keeps reminding us that the report on the non-story is the result of a "team report."

The maddening aspect of local news programs with the yin and yang of male and female "teams" is that they are forced to look so interested about upcoming news that has usually been in the can for hours before air time. This "bit" is as follows:

The man starts with the exciting news that, "Today there was still another fire in the three hundred block of Elm Street." Protocol demands that the male, then, turn to his female partner and look at her with intense interest as she begins to read her portion of the story off the Teleprompter with breathless abandon, even though she has been rehearsing this item for quite some time. Then the female chimes in with, "That's right, Rock, there was, indeed, a fire at the three hundred block of Elm Street and several fire trucks responded to the scene of the blaze. In fact, our crack reporter, Phil Fogarty, is there as we speak, ready with a live report. Phil, tell us about it."

Is that exciting or what?

VI

TORO MERDE

Comedian George Carlin is very perceptive. He can trash just about any subject under the sun and usually does on his periodic HBO specials. He has a laser-like ability to spot phoniness a mile away. It should come as no surprise that he has done just this to the news gathering arm of television. What follows is a paraphrased version of a piece that appears in his book, *Brain Droppings*. The paraphrase form is used here to avoid being "Barniclized."*

First, Carlin notes that American media have a thing about the past. This is very true. It reminds me of the increasingly frequent reports of impending doom to be caused by terrible hurricanes heading our way. Usually the local news stations begin reporting these havocs-to-come as soon as the first breeze stirs in the Palm trees on some island about three thousand miles from the U.S. mainland. The reporting style used to tell the world about these horrific winds is invariably of the "The sky is falling" school of journalism. Soon after the first report that all hell is about to break loose, we are taken to "Hurricane Central" to listen to an expert explain just how bad the storm will be. At no time does the expert—and certainly not the local TV news "team", say something like, "You know, this could turn out to be a little bit of nothing, especially if the hurricane-force winds are downgraded to a tropical storm." While there is no actual footage available of this latest horror-to-be, viewers are treated to film, of past hurricanes, really bad ones. Usually the film shows genuine tragedies and horrific winds and damage that struck decades earlier. A cartoon in The New Yorker said it all: The drawing showed a television reporter speaking into a microphone, his hand holding his hat on. His cameraman is filming it all. A lifeguard sits relaxed in his chair above this scene. Behind the reporter is a couple in swim suits waving at the camera. They, too, are relaxed and smiling. The water is calm. The caption read: "The relatively placid seas and those vacationers behind me notwithstanding, Dan, it's really starting to blow out here."

Anyway, Carlin's point about the media's obsession with the past is confirmed by the omnipresent "Anniversaries" that seem to crop up on television most evenings of any given week. For instance, how many times have you seen one or more of the following "Anniversaries": Jack Kennedy's life and death; Bobby Kennedy's life and death; Martin Luther King's life and death; World War II (strangely not much on Korea and Vietnam); Princess Diana's life and death; the 1968 Democratic convention in Chicago with the obligatory shots of Mayor John Daly tossing profanity at Senator Abe Ribicoff, who was at the lectern trying to give a speech; the dropping of the first atomic bomb on Hiroshima; the Beatles's first visit to the United States; the life and death of Elvis. On and on it goes. If you missed it the first or tenth time around, don't worry, it will definitely show up again, so watch your local listings.

Carlin is at his best when he calls our attention to a practice of TV news "teams" that, really, should have had us at the barricades shouting, "We're mad as hell, and we're not going to take it anymore!" long before now. What he describes is something we've all sat through for years and continue to sit through without even trying to throw a shoe at the TV screen:

He begins by noting that these TV news shows avoid living in the present by announcing all of those "Anniversaries" coming up and constantly telling us to keep an eye on what's coming up next: You know them all: "Still to come," "Stay with us," "Still ahead," and so on. He notes that they even preview what's coming up an hour later. For example: The TV newscaster on the five o'clock program tells us that Harry Barf who does the six o'clock news will take a moment to tell us what is coming up on the six o'clock show. This is always open to question because, as Carlin says, if the guy on the five o'clock program were any kind of newsman, *he'd* tell us what that news is so we wouldn't have to wait around. Hell, we could go out to a movie or mow the lawn or do something constructive instead of waiting for the news at six o'clock. The absurdity of it all builds as a news person in the morning tells us what's going to be reported that evening! Hey, we can't wait, right?

It goes without saying that Carlin doesn't overlook the fact that those six o'clock news mavens who are anxiously awaiting for the two hands to reach 12 and six are in shirt sleeves, sleeves usually rolled up. We even see those multi-million dollar guys, Jennings, Brokaw and Rather in their shirt sleeves, busily refining all of those non-news stories they have had in the can for hours. I'll be up front about this and admit that I, too, would appear in shirt sleeves if they paid me a few million a year to read from a Teleprompter. Hell, I'd do it in the buff.

* * *

* Bill Barnicle was a columnist for the *Boston Globe* for about 25 years, penning thousands of stories. He made the mistake of using some of Carlin's *Brain Droppings* material without attributing any of it to the comedian. The *Globe*, which had recently fired a black, female reporter for fudging on her facts, told Barnicle he must go. He was taken back a day or so later, but when it turned up that he had fudged some facts in a column done many years before, he had to say Sayonara. **

** A former editor of *The Reader's Digest* called the Globe's attention to the incident.***

*** Barnicle was later hired to be a television commentator on a Boston station, so now his recognition factor will finally go through the roof and he won't have to lower his handsome standard of living.

VII

SPORTS SCHMORTS

One only has to watch a sports event on British television to realize how downright infantile are American broadcasters who pass themselves off as sports experts. A convincing argument was made for this conclusion when my wife and I were in London a few years ago when Martina Navritalova and Steffi Graf met in the final of the U.S. Open Tennis Championship.

Exhausted from walking all day in London Town and eating large amounts of unbelievably tasty food, we relaxed in our hotel room. We turned on the *Telly* and realized that our country's tennis championship was being contested by Martina and Steffi. (Only in America would a German and a native Czech, be vying for the U.S. title.) Yes, Virginia, we are tennis buffs. We turned on the set in time

31

to watch the climax of the truly exciting last set. Steffi should have won but she didn't. She had every opportunity to take the title away from the aging but still extremely capable Navritalova. There must have been a half dozen match points against Martina. Steffi couldn't pull it off as the defending champion fought off defeat time and time again. Finally after some of the most exciting tennis we'd ever seen, Martina had another title under her chemise.

The point, you ask: At no time during the roughly 10 minutes of total excitement and touch and go play taking place on the court, did the BBC announcers raise their voices. They very calmly commented on the match, without repeating for the listeners's benefit every facet of every point. My wife and I commented how pleasant it was to have relative quiet as we watched the match unfold. The BBC broadcasters obviously gave us the benefit of the doubt about seeing points being made and assumed that having seen each point, we did not require a blow-by-blow recap of what it was we had just witnessed a second or two before.

Compare this experience with the BBC with what we view here at home. On an average local television station, we have co-anchors (almost always a man and a woman, and in industrial cities there is one white and one black), a weather person, and a sports announcer. It is impossible not to notice the difference between these *professionals.* The co-anchors usually deliver the news to us with breathless enthusiasm, even when the stories they deliver are the usual non-news stories. The weather person does a lot of pointing and tries to sound as profound as possible as he or she tells us what the U.S. Weather Service told them a few hours before. Then the three "team" members turn their heads, smile and look at the sports member of the team. There is usually a bit of light banter at this juncture. They kid each other and make terrible jokes. They chuckle a lot.

The first thing a viewer notices is that the sports guy is pumped up. His voice is totally macho. His chest heaves in and out as he intones in a brutally masculine voice what occurred that day in the world of sports, even when hardly anything happened that day in the world of sports. It is as if the sports announcer, just before the camera zooms in on him, has done a mantra to himself that goes something like, "Pump yourself up baby and get ready to rock and roll! It's show time!" The sports announcer's voice must be slangy and delivered with bravado and great intensity.

Where did all this begin? The machismo school of sports broadcasting probably began in the days before television. Ted Husing and Bill Stern made football games that radio listeners couldn't see come alive. Their enthusiastic calling of games put us all in seats on the 50 yard line. Red Barber, Harry Carey and Mel Allen did the same for baseball fans who couldn't sneak away from work to go to the ballpark. Don Dunphy brought a Joe Louis championship bout into our living rooms and you could almost smell the sweat. Announcing games listeners could not see made for understandable intensity on the part of sports broadcasters in the pre-TV days. They were adding to their radio-bound audience's enjoyment of what it was they were describing.

Enter television. Apparently no one told TV sports announcers that there was an obvious difference between radio and the tube. The viewers actually see what the announcer sees at the same time. There is, therefore, no need to call attention to every detail of a game or a match. Because no one told them this, announcers feel obligated to tell viewers every detail of what it is they are watching. When women began to invade the previously all-male sports broadcasting domain, the female hired for the job was apparently told that the first order of business, a la Henry Higgins's plaint, was to try to sound as much as possible like a man, preferably like a man on amphetamines. In short, the woman should try as best she can to exude machismo!

There are very few exceptions to this observation. John McEnroe, certainly one of the all-time great tennis players, comments on what he is watching with calm objectivity. Conversely, Barry McKay, no slouch as a player years ago, describes action on the court as if he is reporting on the first match he's ever seen. "Wow," "Boy" and other choice exclamations are made regularly by this ex- champion. If a person has been a champion, is it likely that he or she will describe a well executed drop volley by saying something like, "Wow, it really didn't look like he was even going to reach the ball, let alone hit that shot with the accuracy we just saw!" Unlikely.

Ex-football players are the worst. Former Super Bowl champion quarterbacks or linebackers or running backs begin a pre-game analysis as if they have returned to childhood. They slap the desk enthusiastically, make terrible jokes about what they are wearing that day, and *always* fail to behave as if they are adults. Rule No. 1 seems to be that no football expert is to make any comment without motioning with his hands as if the studio is infested with mosquitoes. There are exceptions, but not many.

"**Journalists, like lawyers and members of Congress, have become the sort of people ordinary folks just love to hate. In movies and TV shows they're portrayed as obnoxious busybodies who are always sticking microphones in people's faces. And there are certainly enough real-life examples to support that negative image.**"

David Ignatius
Washington Post

VIII

ARREST THOSE PHOTOGRAPHERS!

The tragic death of Princess Diana did nothing to stop the practice of photographers besieging any one unfortunate enough to have a face that can bring a good price in the media marketplace.

For a few days following her death in a Paris tunnel, there was an outcry that condemned the herd of photographers who may or may not have contributed to the accident that took her life. The *Paparazzi* were named as possible co-executioners. There was general agreement that something should be done to avoid similar tragedies in the future. No way Jose. About a year later, a young woman by the name of Monica Lewinski came in for her 15 minutes-plus of fame. There were many examples of photojournalistic excesses, but the most disturbing example came when Monica and her father were shown leaving a Los Angeles restaurant on the way to their car. They could just hardly move! Photographers surrounded them, pressing in so close that they could barely move forward. They finally got to their car and got in, but in no way thanks to the photographers. ("Boo" and "hiss" as well to the reporters present with their omnipresent recorders shoved in the faces of the harried Lewinskis.)

When Princess Diana died, criticism was leveled at *Paparazzi*, those independent photographers who circle the globe in search of a picture that they can sell for a high price to photographic services who sell pictures to magazines, newspapers, television and whoever else will pay. These are the folk responsible for a photograph of Jackie Onassis stark naked on a Greek isle. These photographers are not above heckling their targets, trying to have them react—preferably violently, to give them the most marketable picture. Princess Diana frequently described this and other ploys the cameramen used to taunt her into marketable reactions. She said that some eager cameramen would talk to her as she walked outside, trying to get her to react in a way to give the photographer an unusual and, therefore, more marketable shot. "Come on Di, give us a good look, give us a scowl; that's a good girl. I've got a kid in private school and you'll help me pay the bills," she related to an interviewer.

But many of the photographers in Los Angeles and elsewhere are employees of various media, not self employed independents. In fact, most scenes of photographer excesses in this country are of paid cameramen and women employed by various media. What is not explained to the general public is that a photographer for the *New York Daily News*, for example, can market a shot the *News* does not use to any photographic service who is willing to pay for it. In fact, photographers for newspapers could well be some of the highest paid people anywhere.

If photographers were not solely responsible for the breakup of the marriage of Madonna and Sean Penn, they were probably corespondents, to say the very least. Tabloids featured many photographs of Penn throwing a punch at some photographer who had actually taunted him into throwing that punch. Scenes such as these were re-enacted almost daily. The Penns couldn't make a move without being hassled by photographers who were out to make a buck. Do we assume that photographers cared about what stress might do to the marriage of these celebrities? Hardly.

This situation of the photographic herd instinct is nothing new. Any movie that contains a scene of a harried witness leaving a courthouse will have an obligatory situation with scores of cameras in the face of the witness attempting to get into an awaiting automobile.

Ron Valella is a name that is probably best known for having some restraint placed upon the way photographers go after human paydays. Jackie Onassis's picture showed up in virtually every publication on earth. The photographer who sold many of those photos to various magazines and newspapers was Ron Valella. Some enterprising photographers even made money by taking photos of Valella taking a picture of Ms. Onassis. At last, a judge placed a restraining order on Valella, requiring him to stay a minimum distance away from her. The restraining order applied only to Valella. It obviously had no effect on those who made it almost impossible for Ms. Lewinski and her family to walk to their car.

Michael J. O'Neill, former editor of the *New York Daily News,* recognized the need to restrain photographers from making life so unpleasant for so many. In one of his last speeches before his retirement, he called attention to the practice of creating a mob scene when someone in the news walks about in public. O'Neill suggested that certain limits should be placed on photographers, such as minimum distances between them and their subjects. (And this from a long-time editor of a tabloid!) Such a restriction seems to make sense and is certainly long overdue when one considers today's modern equipment that allows high quality pictures to be taken from great distances.

It seems to make sense, but O'Neill gave that speech in the early 1980s. Since that time there has been nothing done to end the in-your-face approach to photo journalism.

IX

NON-JOURNALIST JOURNALISTS

The definition of what a journalist is covers a broad spectrum. Generally it has to do with writing, editing and/or publishing newspapers, magazines and other news and opinion publications. Added to this during the second half of the 20th century was anyone reporting news on television, and even later via Internet web sites that report on damn near anything. Mention that someone is a journalist and the assumption is that he or she works for a news publication or broadcast entity in a writing or editing capacity. If a person is a press operator for a newspaper, that person is a press operator and is not considered a journalist. A person who sits at a copy desk all day and edits or writes items to go into a publication is a journalist. However, in the broad sense, that sedentary operative at a newspaper is not thought of when someone uses the term because it usually refers to someone who writes the material that is read by those who read the publication. Similarly, an on-air television reporter would be considered a journalist, while his or her cameraman (woman) would not, although there is that quaint phrase, "photo-journalist." Ask Mike Wallace or Ed Bradley of *60 Minutes* what he is and "journalist" will probably be the reply. Ask Don Hewitt, the producer of Wallace's program what he is and "TV producer" would probably be his answer, although he has worked with Murrow and the current gang for many years and is responsible for much of what has gone on the air of quality.

Several journalists are writing about journalists these days and the writing is not exactly generous. *Washingtonian Magazine once* had an article that praised journalists of the past. The writer lauded past journalists. He began the article by saying that many polls show that "journalists stink." He then went on to write about H.L. Mencken, A.J. Leibling, Teddy White and others who have written great journalism, usually against tight deadlines and frequently under immense pressure such as during a war.

Historically, a journalist was someone who got out of college (or high school in the days of H.L. Mencken) and got a job as a newspaper reporter. They liked to write and to be a witness to events. Depending on his or her ability, that person moved up to increasingly important news "beats" and, if really outstanding, became an editor who ceased to write much, but, instead edited or directed the work of reporters.

Since television, the definition of what a journalist is has changed considerably. Edward R. Murrow, one of the most famous "journalists" in history, had no newspaper or broadcasting experience before he was tapped by CBS during World War II to head its overseas team of radio broadcasters. He was simply a natural with a voice that became his signature when he intoned, "This…is London," during the battle of Britain. He was at the right place at exactly the right time. He wound up hiring several men who became CBS stalwarts such as Eric Sevareid.

At present, probably since the O.J. Simpson trial, the trend has changed considerably. Many of the omnipresent guests or hosts on so-called TV talk shows these days are lawyers who are brought out nightly to give a legal overview of the *Topic du jour*. Jeffrey Toobin, of *The New Yorker*, and Stuart Taylor of the *National Journal* are typical of the relatively young persons who did well in law school (Taylor was editor of Harvard's prestigious Law Review) and wound up as experts used to explain legal details to the non-legal viewers by various networks. They are seen frequently on various talk shows. Toobin has even landed a spot as Good Morning America's legal "advisor." During the Clinton-Lewinski period Chris Matthews seldom made a move without turning to Taylor for his low keyed explanations of things legal. Greta Van Susteren and Roger Cossack were used as CNN legal analysts during the Simpson trial. They caught on with a legal minded audience and were given their own show, *Burden of Proof*, on CNN. It seems that these and other lawyers who may or may not have ever written a story on deadline for a newspaper or magazine, are the new generation of journalists. Toobin and Taylor write for magazines and appear on TV talk shows, having given up, it seems, any idea of practicing the law. It is not known whether Van Susteren and Cossack have ever written anything other than legal briefs. It does prompt one to ask just when either of them finds the time to ply their still active legal trade.

There is a theory making the rounds (it began just now) that lawyers have banded together to keep legal cases a'comin. The O.J. Simpson trial started things off by keeping millions riveted to their TV sets each day to watch the trial, itself, and, then, tune in Geraldo Rivera, Charles Grodin and others in the evening to witness unending analysis of what transpired that day in the court room. Geraldo seemed to have lawyers showing up with a frequency that reminded one of the Volkswagen at the circus that disgorges scores of clowns to the bewilderment of those in attendance. Grodin simply hammered Simpson's legal Dream Team mercilessly. He called Johnny Cochran a liar almost nightly. Before CNBC made room for him, Grodin was a full-time film actor, with no previous on-air experience except as a guest on one of the late night talk shows.

So, soon after the Simpson trial came to an end, the Lewinski scandal hit the fan and lawyers, once again, appeared on talk shows at every opportunity. In fact, Rivera has been going non-stop on one crisis or another since O.J. swore he was totally innocent of killing his wife and her friend. Once the Clinton scandals passed, there were others to take its place, such as the still-unsolved murder of Jon-Benet Ramsey. There will, henceforth, probably be some other media event that will keep Americans in front of their TVS and lawyers doing their interpretive thing before the camera.

Journalists used to be profane, heavy drinking and usually good writers. Today's journalists, even those with solid newspaper backgrounds, are opting to be television personalities. Let's ask a rhetorical question: If the following "journalists" who appear regularly on various television talk shows had to choose between television or their newspaper or magazine jobs, which would they give up? Mark Shields and Paul Gigot, regulars on PBS's Jim Lehrer News Hour; Jonathan Alter, *Newsweek* columnist who appears on Geraldo and other programs frequently enough to be considered a regular; Fred Barnes, editor of the relatively new *Weekly Standard* and a regular on the McLaughlin Group and Fox News. Then there's Tony Snow, conservative columnist who earned his journalistic stripes working in the White House. There are scores of others who seem to pop up on various talk shows almost daily. Again, would any of these "personalities" give up the glamour of being on television and return to only appearing in public via the written word?

Hardly.

Howard Kurtz, perceptive media analyst for the *Washington Post,* identified the problem with today's crop of journalists in an article, entitled, *Attitude Sickness.* Kurtz cited a conclusion made by maverick journalist James Fallows, who had just been ousted as editor of *U.S. News & World Report.* Apparently Fallows believes reporters these days are simply uninterested in what they are reporting and, therefore, turn out uninteresting journalism. This is especially true of the political-writer class because, Fallows noted, they are shallow, incurious and hold a cynical view of life.

Kurtz mentioned another editor who claims that print journalists just don't know what to do because of the dominance of television. *Newsweek's* Jonathan Alter is reported as admitting that old-time "stenographic" reporting is below the ambitions of today's print journalists who hope against hope that they go on TV to analyze the news as Alter does on NBC. Years ago, budding journalists were taught to adhere to the *inverted pyramid* rule. This rule made it mandatory for a reporter to put the most important item or items (who, what, when, where, and why) in the first few paragraphs and less important information later in the piece. This practice was followed because if a story had to be cut in length from the bottom, an editor didn't risk eliminating important details. The reporter's opinion was not to be found in any news piece. Today's ambitious print journalists understandably bridal at the prospect of reporting just the facts. By reporting only the facts, how in the world is a guy or gal supposed to wind up on television and cash in on the celebrity and money that goes with that territory? Being on television and known as opposed to being in print and relatively unknown also means greater access to those lucrative speaking engagements that pay those huge honoraria.

X

MEDIA REALITY

Print and broadcast media are not what they seem. The first newspapers probably were a mishmash of items such as "Ship Arrivals and Ship Departures," announcements of political matters such as elections, news of barn raisings and calls for volunteers and the like. As time passed, cartoons appeared as well as editorial opinions on a variety of matters. Later, owners of newspapers such as William Randolph Hearst tried to provoke the country into war and, later, attempted to influence foreign policy as Henry Luce did relentlessly with regard to Time Magazine's love affair with China.

Radio took hold and the likes of Westbrook Pegler and Walter Winchell felt free to throw their weight around and virtually directed much of this nation's foreign and domestic policy simply by influencing public opinion. Too, radio brought World War II (and Murrow's voice) into American homes.

Television began with Uncle Miltie and soon promoted Murrow and other radio celebrities to pundits who could give the nation its ration of news as well as produce programs that brought into living rooms civil rights obscenities, historical vignettes such as Walter Cronkite's *You Are There,* and Murrow's *See It Now*, which was able to help bring the curtain down on McCarthyism.

And so it went. Television evolved into a little of this—sitcoms and *Monday Night Football*, and a little of that—*Masterpiece Theater*, *Roots, Glory* and other uplifting and educational programming. Broadcast news developed from newspapers and/or wire service stories, read on air as a *News Program* to today's mixture of All-News, Talk, Local and Network news on the hour and half hour. Locally, traffic reports and weather demand a healthy portion of any news report.

With the advent of Matt Drudge on the Internet, traditional media have criticized this Runyanesque upstart (no college!) who commands too much attention. Mainstream journalists have frequently criticized Drudge for reporting items without double checking their accuracy, something that is merchandised as something mainstream media do as a matter of policy. The practice of double checking sources was apparently established as journalistic gospel by the *Washington Post* during its famous coverage of Watergate. Drudge repels such criticism by citing instances where mainstream media have rushed stories into print or on the air without checking the credibility of anything, namely the plethora of stories that flooded television and print when Drudge made Monica Lewinski a household name. Let us not forget that many decades of great journalism was produced long before the *Post* made double sourcing the thing to do.

Whence the news? Years ago, a news announcer on radio, gave listeners news gathered from the AP or UP wires at the radio station. Using very subjective selectivity he (there were no shes) sometimes read a story straight from that day's local newspaper. Any person could have done this and in many cases, just about any person at a radio station did. As time passed, a high school education no longer was sufficient to be a journalist. David Brinkley got in under the radar and others managed to do it, but, generally speaking, the higher the education the better the chance of becoming a reporter or, in the case of law school graduates, becoming instant syndicated columnists.

The rivalry between print and television journalists is real and ongoing. This is understandable. If a man or woman is a hard working print journalist who occasionally covers a story that warrants a by-line, maybe on the first page, chances are few people outside his or her immediate family could pick them out in a police lineup. The television news readers get all the recognition. This is a fact of life, as demonstrated by film stars. Many stars have commented that they hardly ever were recognized in public. But once they appear on a television sit-com, they find it almost impossible to go out in public without being hailed by passersby. When I was a promotion operative for the *New York Daily News*, I remember as if it were 10 minutes ago, an example of the television-press rivalry. The *News* was very close to closing its doors forever. Times were tough for what had been the largest circulation newspaper in the nation. During one period there were almost daily rumors that the News was *that* close to losing the battle for News Yorkers's affection to the *Post*, Television crews were frequently posted outside the famous art deco headquarters of the *News*. Fed up with the constant uncertainty, a News editor was incensed enough to walk up to a television reporter and scream, "You bastards wouldn't have a thing to report if we go out of business. All you do is report every day what you read in our paper."

That is not far from the truth. A television reporter or editor probably begins his or her working day by reading at least one and probably several newspapers, from which is gleaned potential news stories to go after that day. Actually, newspaper and magazine editors do much the same thing. If a significant story appears in *The New York Times*, chances are an editor at the *Washington Post*, or *L.A. Times*, or *Chicago Tribune* will assign a reporter to do a story on the story that the *Times* broke. If the truth be known, these days, most editors, reporters and anyone with access to a computer probably checks in on *The Drudge Report* to get a feel for what should be covered that day.

One only has to examine how many front page stories a newspaper carries that are attributed to a wire service to gauge the quality of that publication. One can gauge the professionalism of a television news program by watching how a man or woman delivers the news. It is relatively easy to spot an air head.

Why is it that local television news is so happy. Network news tries to be, well, profound. Jennings, Rather and the others, intone the news as if they are atop Mt. Rushmore (or maybe Mt. Sinae) giving us the news or non-news as seriously as they can. After all, they are supposed to be serious purveyors of what we are supposed to learn each day. But compare this to those local morning or evening or late evening news shows (note that the word program was not used) where everyone on camera seems to be as happy as those kids in Ovaltine commercials. I mean they are almost spastically happy.

On comes the woman, smiling to beat the band and seemingly ecstatic about being on air to read us whatever passes as news that day. But, first, she must smile, read about a sentence or two of what's comin' at us, then turn smilingly to her co-host (always the opposite gender) and give him a chance to tell us his name and give us still another parcel of what's to be presented during the next 22-minus minutes.

They are almost giggly. The weather person has been waiting around so long that he or she almost is in tears of gratitude when they get a chance to do their "thing." We have heard umpteen versions of that day's weather and the next day, but the weather "expert" dances around in front of those weather maps as if they are auditioning for "All That Jazz." Every movie ever made has made fun of television news reporters. There must be a reason for this. Maybe it's because they are so damn laughable. They are cartoon characters. But they make much more money than they would shuffling papers in an office so they opt to shuffle papers before a television audience LIVE!!!

XI

INTERVIEWS WE HAVE KNOWN

Who knows how it all began? Maybe it was Edward R. Murrow who slipped down from his lofty perch above American journalism and started interviewing all sorts of celebrities through clouds of cigarette smoke. Murrow tossed friendly softball questions at his *Celebrity du le Semain* as he took Americans into the homes of film stars and anyone else who might have a bit of star dust sprinkled on them.

Since Murrow passed from the scene, Barbara Walters has made interviewing celebrities a fine art. She is undoubtedly the premier television interviewer. Invariably, Ms Walters gets her subjects to break into sobs by asking questions so personal that the interviewee simply remembers thoughts so sad and terrible to open the floodgates as if on command. Ms. Walters also asks such penetrating questions as "If you were a tree…" which has become famous and a trademark of hers. During any given interview, ABC's doyen of interviewing reeks of concern and sincerity. Her expression is exactly what a Hollywood film director would call for of an actor who had just entered a funeral home's viewing room.

Giving Barbara Walters a run for her money (scads of it!) is Diane Sawyer, another ABC star. No one on the face of the earth exudes as much syrupy seriousness as does Ms. Sawyer. Her approach to questioning makes Ms. Walters's style appear downright giddy by comparison. Ms. Walters shows concern mainly via her voice, with an occasional, obligatory raised eyebrow to denote concern. Diane Sawyer utilizes both voice and ever moving eyebrows to become one with an interviewee. Interviewing the 1998-1999 Whipping Boy of the Year (s), Kenneth Starr, Ms. Sawyer employed every expression in her impressive arsenal. She looked so serious while asking questions that a casual viewer might have feared that she was about to physically attack Starr at any moment. "People say that you are…" she would say, leveling an accusation, based on the latest headline. "It is said you sing hymns while out jogging," she intoned incredulously, as if by doing so Starr violated her personal code of conduct while trying to stay fit. It was an all-out attack on the Independent Counsel, an attack that made any observer feel sorry for Starr and almost afraid of Ms. Sawyer.

Journalists as well as non-journalists are getting into the apparently lucrative interviewing game. Connie Chung keeps losing her job by asking indelicate questions. Somehow she rises from the ashes to land another high paying spot on still another network. Her interviewing style is basically just serious without the theatrical facial expressions employed by ABC's Walters-Sawyer battery.

Programs such as ABC's *Good Morning America* and NBC's *Today* have personalities who do a lot of interviewing. *Good Morning America* had a good run as Number 1, with Joan Lunden and Charles Gibson capable of conducting effective interviews. A replacement duo, Lisa McRee and Kevin Newman, bit the dust because they failed to boost ABC's, by then, sagging morning ratings. Interviews by them were said to lack focus and appeared to be scripted to give offense to the interviewee and, therefore, became controversial which never hurt a show in trouble. (Gibson and Diane Sawyer were hustled back, temporarily, by ABC to stop the slippage at the beginning of 1999.As this is written in 2002, they are still there.) During Gumbel's reign he asked questions of guests that bordered on inflammatory. It wouldn't have been surprising if a guest got up and left or, if Gumbel went too far, suggesting fisticuffs as an alternative. Katie Couric may be small, but she delivers a solid punch to anyone she is interviewing, especially, it seems, anyone of the conservative stripe. The diminutive Couric always gives the impression of questioning the veracity of a guest. She frequently appears to be almost belligerent. She recently renewed her contract for an obscene amount of money.

Interviewing has even been suggested as a possible alternative to engaging in public policy. Larry King once suggested in all seriousness that, perhaps, President Clinton could have made everything right with the American people concerning Ms. Lewinski by appearing on his show "for the whole hour." What Congress had not been able to do, King assumed he could do.

Only in America.

XII

WHAT IS A JOURNALIST?

Cable television isn't what it seems. The all-news-all-day-long-and-then-some channels such as CNN, CNBC, MSNBC, FOX News, and the like reach a relatively small audience. Radio's Rush Limbaugh regularly denigrates *Larry King Live* by claiming that King reaches fewer than one million households, a small number compared to the number of viewers watching network sitcoms, movies, evening news, and so on. However, apparently King does reach a healthy segment of thought leaders, judging by the array of thought leaders who appear on his show.

C-Span and various other cable outlets seem to televise an inordinate number of panel discussion programs that deal with how well professional journalists do their job. It is as if these panel shows are conducted almost daily. The panelists are often the same on these shows. (A tangential viewer's *bonus* occurred one day when Morley Safer of CBS's *60 Minutes* was seen smoking a cigarette while in a building that, these days, would almost certainly be a non-smoking building. Apparently Safer just had to have a smoke and no one said a word.)

These discussion shows usually have panelists who have earned their journalistic stripes, paid their dues and have been around for some time. Whatever their original entry level into the world of journalism, today they are usually highly paid writers, many of whom are syndicated columnists or broadcast celebrities such as Safer. The panel subjects usually range from topics such as, "Is there really a liberal bias in reporting the news?" to something like, "Is there too much un-sourced reporting getting into newspapers and on the air?"

The answer to both questions is an obvious, "Yes." Panelists, however, talk endlessly about there not being a liberal bias and that mainstream journalists always make certain that stories are properly sourced but that, yes, there are tabloids and cyberspace journalist wannabes such as Matt Drudge who muddy the waters from time to time by reporting unsubstantiated stories.

Let's take Matt Drudge as a paradigm of someone who, on paper, is unqualified to call himself a journalist. He has had no college experience and does seem to report items as he hears of them, without checking out their accuracy first. Notwithstanding this lack of proper credentials, Drudge's web page is said to receive far more "Hits" than most other media web pages. He just seems to have a lot of newsy material that bonafide journalists seem to like to check out while they have their morning coffee.

Most cities are said to be one-newspaper towns these days, unlike years ago when many cities had at least two papers, usually a liberal and a conservative option. There are many hundreds of newspapers in the country. There are relatively few first-rate newspapers. Once one ticks off the usual premier papers, most of the other newspapers lack in-depth quality and resort to a great deal of wire service material to fill even their front page.

So, Let's assume that the *New York Times, New York Daily News, Newsday, L.A. Times. Chicago Tribune, Chicago Sun Times, Boston Globe, San Francisco Examiner, Wall Street Journal, Washington Post, Miami Herald, Atlanta Journal & Constitution, Baltimore Sun, Detroit Free Press, Kansas City Star, Philadelphia Inquirer* and a few other papers are considered first rate. The assumption is that they hire only the *creme de la creme* coming out of journalism schools or top-rung universities such as Harvard and Yale. This appears to be analogous to the hiring practices of top law firms. A law degree from Harvard and Yale brings a new hiree a top salary and the brightest of futures. A law school graduate from a lesser institution might be twice the lawyer as his or her Harvard or Yale counterpart, but probably will never be given the opportunity to prove it.

We know what the future probably holds for the Harvard graduate who enters the world of work by joining the staff of *Time* or *The New*

York Times. For starters there will be a ticket into Expense Account Heaven and important assignments with which to hone his or her talents. In time, this journalist will either rise to an enviable level within AOL-Time-Warner or will write a book that will sell well. They will leave the world of magazines and write a syndicated column and make lots of money and appear on television talk shows and attend Gridiron Dinners and the like. But what of the young graduate from a small liberal arts college who was editor of the school paper and who wants to be a journalist in the worst way? He or she might be happy to land a job as a reporter for the *Biloxi Bugle*, covering high school basketball and weekly council meetings at the town hall. Level of pay will be modest, tied to Guild salary standards and there will be no $100 lunches for two. Stories will be essentially boring to cover and write, but this potential Pulitzer Prize winner will earn valuable journalistic spurs. Alas, this journalist, now married and the father of a baby boy, will drop out after about five years and take a position with a public relations firm and earn a decent salary for the first time. He or she will cease to be a journalist. They will spend the rest of their lives watching lawyer-journalists strut their stuff on nationally televised panel shows.

The term journalist covers a wide area of endeavor. A person who goes straight to work for a magazine never gets to enjoy the special sounds and smells of a press room. Copy is written and sent to some far off printing plant by computer. Most men and women who work in editorial positions for national magazines wear expensive clothes.

This journalist is primarily a *Writer*, not even a Reporter. He or she could be a specialist in science or sports or technology or politics. In time the term "Expert" can be applied. Virtually everything written by the Writer will be edited before becoming part of the publication.

The journalist for a newspaper will go out and about covering news stories. Little editing will be done on what is turned in to a copy desk. While writing news stories, this reporter will probably stay up late writing material he or she hopes to freelance. This is done to make additional money and hopefully break out of the dead end job in which he or she finds themselves.

So how do we judge who does or does not have adequate credentials to report a story? Reporters are often around other reporters during much of the working day, as demonstrated by those scenes in the White House press briefing room where reporters hang out for a good part of the day, waiting to be told what they will report. Example of how it can work: Reporter A shows up sleepy eyed in the Senate Press Dining Room for a small breakfast. Other reporters are there, chatting. The late arrival eases into his or her coffee and hears other reporters opining that they are concerned about the weather ruining their weekend plans. There seems to be a consensus on this matter. Later, the reporter files a story that begins:

"Capitol Hill sources have expressed concern about the weather this weekend. Some say it could ruin weekend plans for many…"

That story has been "Sourced" by at least two other journalists over corn bread and coffee. This method of reporting is age old and nothing is deemed to be wrong with it. But if Matt Drudge gets three phone calls telling him the same details about the same subject he is dismissed by mainstream media as being irresponsible.

There is an interesting phenomenon that has been around for years. It occurs frequently. This happens when an important political figure will be "interviewed" or questioned by a group of grammar school or high school youngsters. It is not unusual for the politician to say something like, "You know, those kids asked better questions than members of the press corps." Such a reaction comes as no surprise. Listen in to a C-Span or CNN coverage of a White House press briefing by the Press Secretary of the moment. Questioning begins with a series of somewhat relevant questions and soon begins to flag. Questions come from the reporters who have been hanging out for hours waiting for someone to talk to. It seems as if inane questions will continue to be asked as long as the Press Secretary remains at the podium. Even when the President is at the podium, questions begin seriously and, inevitably, a tone of humor becomes apparent and "kidding around" is the order of the day. This reflects the basic comraderie that exists between the President and those covering him. There are exceptions, as when Richard Nixon was President and challenged the integrity of the press corps that covered him and his administration. A few reporters tried to hit Clinton hard, but he simply refused to answer, saying he was too busy doing the people's business to do so.

The diminished quality of the Washington Press Corps was exposed during the Gulf War. Daily press briefings were held at the Pentagon, led by a general officer assigned to give a daily overview and answer questions. The questions soon made it clear that those asking the questions had a loose grasp of military terminology, not to mention technology. It is interesting that the shallowness of military knowledge among the questioners was reported by various media, noting that many in the Pentagon briefing room didn't know enough about what they were being told about the Gulf War to ask intelligent questions. Yet the biggest story to come out of the war from the media's point of view was that the military forces in the Gulf limited media access to the battle zone, itself. Seeing as how most U.S. casualties during the Gulf War were from friendly fire, it is probably a good thing that reporters were not allowed too close to the actual battle area.

Basic arithmetic would indicate that a relatively small number of journalists enter print or broadcast news operations from journalism schools. One must ask, then, whether journalism school alumni represent qualified journalists and those who become reporters and have only on-the-job training are not as qualified to report the news. Such a conclusion would mean that the vast majority of news that turns up in newspapers and on the air is prepared and delivered by operatives with meager credentials. The only problem with this line of reasoning is that reporters from non-journalism colleges frequently turn out to be better than those with blue ribbon resumes. Life can be unfair indeed.

"A variety of studies, surveys and focus groups document a real resentment of the press and its practice among Americans, who characterize the news media as arrogant, inaccurate, superficial, sensational, biased and bent. Worse, they apparently believe that the press is part of the problem, rather than part of the solution."

Paul McMasters
Freedom Forum

XIII

NO NEWS IS NO NEWS

Let's explore further the world of news gathering, the subject of all those cable panel shows that have journalists explaining whether or not they are doing an adequate job of covering the news. So far we have hinted at the lack of excitement in the workday of most journalists. There's a report of insignificance here and a report of even greater insignificance there. Think about it for a moment: How many times in a year do you use a news story as a topic of conversation? Probably not many. There simply isn't much happening in this world of ours that qualifies as news.

Repetition doesn't help either. Anyone old enough remembers the manned launch when Neil Armstrong stepped on the moon, Richard Nixon's impeachment proceedings, the Baltimore Colts-New York

Giants 1958 "Greatest Football Game Ever Played," Bobby Kennedy vs. Eugene McCarthy in 1968, the first few Super Bowls. Well, you get the point. Shuttle flights to who knows where get little attention these days. Still another politician asking voters to give them their hand and help receive a ho hum response. It is difficult to identify many athletes these days even though they are paid guarganuan sums. Polls showed that many Americans were bored stiff from talk about impeaching Bill Clinton. The Gulf War was well received by the public, but lesser military operations such as those in Haiti and Bosnia turned out to be relative yawners. The public easily becomes inured about otherwise exciting events and can focus attention and interest up to a point and no more. This explains why many newspapers resort to huge headlines about non-stories and television anchors try to sound very excited about very dull stories.

The lack of exciting news explains why many news stories are inaccurate and draw criticism for being overblown. This is the reason as well why the media tend to dwell on stories that are, well, juicy. Reporters spend most working days almost bored silly. There just isn't much to report. Oh, they will turn in stories, but they will lack bite, they will not catch anyone's attention. Think about this: Ice hockey comes in for criticism from time to time for being too violent. A television sportscaster had a simple solution years ago during his broadcast. He said that if a hockey player takes off his gloves, he should automatically be ousted from a game. Yet gloves are removed with regularity and fights continue to be an integral part of the game.

The media probably could have ended fighting years ago by mounting a campaign that would have forced a change in the rules. Instead, the media, which counts on exciting ice hockey to help pay the rent via advertising and circulation, have been relatively quiet all this time. The National Hockey League could independently put an end to the fighting by imposing strict rules, but the teams apparently assume that they will lose fans if fighting is banned.

It is obvious. If a reporter covers the Pentagon and there is no war or controversy, how exciting can the Pentagon beat be? If a reporter covers the White House and the world of foreign policy is tranquil and the President doesn't have any international travel plans and there is no domestic controversy how exciting can that White House beat be? But let there be an uprising in Bangladesh and Dan Rather, Peter Jennings and Tom Brokaw will grab their safari jackets out of moth balls like *that*. They and other reporters will have something to report, something to excite them. David Halberstam and other reporters who covered Vietnam, wearing the obligatory safari jackets all the while, have milked that experience for all it is worth. Halberstam and others still show up on panels talking about Vietnam. They write an inordinate number of books about their experiences there. This syndrome is not unlike a soldier's lack of interest in dying but love affair with actual combat. If you think about it, how interesting is it for a military man or women to be on active duty during peacetime?

The O.J. Simpson trial heightened viewer interest in television. Geraldo Rivera and Charles Grodin were given cable shows to capitalize on the attendant interest and excitement in the legal proceedings. The Gulf War had huge numbers of viewers riveted to their sets as daily briefings were given at the Pentagon. The Robert Bork confirmation hearings and the Anita Hill-Clarence Thomas face off had viewers staying up until the wee hours so as not to miss a second of the coverage.

The many Clinton scandals kept many reporters hopping since 1992, but it took Matt Drudge's report on the Internet that this nation's chief executive had been playing doctor with a young intern to breath true excitement into the reporting profession. But, imagine the frustration of being a reporter for a small town weekly newspaper (a journalist, nonetheless) who covers the town council and never had a chance to report anything about Monica and Bill or Anita and Clarence.

It takes tragedy such as assassinations of public officials or floods and earthquakes to make news exciting enough for a journalist to be glad that he or she didn't go into public relations or advertising. It takes high profile murders or exposed corruption at city hall or a football team owner moving a team to another city in the cover of darkness to make a reporter dash to a typewriter or computer. The tragic death of Princess Diana fit the bill in all these categories. She was famous; she died under controversial circumstances and her funeral took place on a world stage. Human emotions were involved so reporters could use adjectives they seldom have an opportunity to use. Mark McGuire and Sammy Sosa gave sports reporters excitement because what they did during the 1998 season was truly exciting.

When a hot story comes along, it is not surprising that reporters frequently get the story wrong. It is almost a requirement that a celebrity who is interviewed to charge when the story appears that the reporter got the quotes all wrong. Inevitably the reporter's editor will make a statement to the effect that, "We stand behind the story as written."

Who's to know, right?

The dearth of real news was confirmed by a survey by the Project for Excellence in Journalism. (This is obviously an on-going project.) The survey took a look at more than 8,000 stories on more than 60 television stations in a cross-section of markets. Most stories ran less than two minutes. At least one station carried stories no longer than 10 seconds! It must be a slow news day, indeed, when a station fills its 22 minutes with little more than a series of sound bytes. It is clear that a typical station develops a menu of just about anything that will fill its allotted time.

XIV

REPORTERS ARE LIKE TICKS

Because the public is easily bored and has seen too many special events too many times, it becomes a reporter's responsibility to search out new news stories. Again, it is easy to imagine how boring a reporter's work day is. This explains why Spiro Agnew ran into a media buzz saw. He happened to utter a phrase that is probably uttered thousands of times every day throughout this land of ours, but not by American Vice Presidents and, especially not by American Vice Presidents who are surrounded by reporters who haven't had anything exciting to report for weeks or even months. Maybe never! It happened during a flight aboard Air Force Two. Agnew was schmoozing with reporters (bored reporters do a lot of schmoozing) when he spotted a Japanese reporter asleep in his seat. Agnew looked down at the sleeping reporter and said something like, "That fat Jap looks comfortable doesn't he?"

That's all it took. Soon, the wire services reported that the Vice President of the United States, the land of the free and the home of the brave, called a Japanese reporter a "Jap." The word, Jap, hasn't been politically correct since John Wayne conquered the Pacific during World War II. The report on what was said actually gave Agnew holy hell because he said something that was, in the reporter's scheme of things, a *no no*. The story implied that no one with any class or taste called a Japanese person a Jap. It was a little early in the game so no one suggested that an independent counsel be named to investigate Agnew.

More recently, former New York Senator Alfonse D'Amato, felt the scorching flames of a reporter who stood as an arbiter of taste. Running for re-election against Congressman Chuck Schumer, D'Amato referred to his opponent as a *Putzhead*. The world soon learned via news reports that putz is Yiddish for penis. D'Amato's reference was equated with radio shock-jock, Howard Stern, calling someone *Dickhead*. D'Amato was forced to apologize and probably lost any chance of being re-elected because he dared to use a phrase that is a Yiddish phrase that is probably used in Jewish areas of New York a few thousand times in any given day. But the report made D'Amato out to be crude and tasteless and, therefore, not worthy of re-election.

Jimmy Carter said in a *Playboy* interview that he lusted in his heart occasionally and committed mental adultery when he spotted a comely damsel. This is a reaction that probably occurs at least millions of times each day among adult males. In fact, it probably is what could be termed a "given". The American media ran with this story as if Carter had confessed to being in violation of the Mann Act! (Without actually saying so, the world knows that Bill Clinton made Jimmy Carter look like a celibate monk when it comes to spotting and appreciating a well turned calf. In fact, if Clinton said he lusted in his heart now and again, it would not even qualify as news.)

Congressman Dan Burton, chairman of a House committee investigating charges against President Clinton, was reported to have called Clinton a "Scumbag." This story went out throughout the land with the same editorial force as news about a nuclear weapon being launched by Saddam Hussein. Soon after Clinton took office, a magazine writer did a profile on Clinton and noted that he was thought to be the first president ever referred by many as a "Scumbag." It is a term that was probably used with some frequency since he took office. Burton's utterance was reported as compromising the objectivity of a committee chairman investigating the President and, therefore, clear indication that Burton was not the proper man for the job. It turned out later, long after Burton had been widely criticized, that a reporter had actually used the term in asking Burton a question during a meeting with a newspaper's editorial board. Not a syllable was ever written or heard about who that reporter happened to be.

The late sports legend, Howard Cosell, got into media hot water by referring to a basketball player of average height as that "little monkey." Nothing wrong with that except the player happened to be black. The reporting of Cosell's utterance made an otherwise objective man who was a close friend of Mohammed Ali out to be a closet bigot. Thus a seemingly innocent comment became on a no-news day, BIG news. It was *not* reported that Cosell often called diminutive white athletes "little monkeys."

Golf pro, Fuzzy Zoeller came face-to-face with the inclination of bored reporters to jump on anything resembling controversy when he made a comment he came to regret when Tiger Woods won the Master's at Augusta National in 1997.

It is the custom at Augusta that the previous year's winner gets to prescribe the menu at the winner's banquet the night before the next year's tournament gets under way. Zoeller is a winner of the famous green jacket and named the menu the year he was the titular host. Walking along the fairway, Zoeller commented that, perhaps, the following year, Woods would call for a meal of fried chicken and collard greens, a clear reference to Woods being an African-American as well as Asian. Predictably, Zoeller was forced to apologize to Woods and Woods had to comment of what Zoeller said and offer his own reaction. The comment by Zoeller had what is called "legs" in show business. The story was kept alive for weeks and is bound to mentioned at least a dozen or so times by some commentator or print reporter each year at the Masters, well, forever.

Probably the most famous politically incorrect utterance was made by Al Campanis, former general manager of the Los Angeles Dodgers baseball team. In a colloquy with reporters, hapless Al said that, in his opinion, blacks were built to excel in some sports such as track, baseball and football, but not swimming. He further opined that, in his opinion, blacks were not made to be front office material for sports teams. He said he wasn't sure exactly why. He just thought God failed to deal them a full deck of mental acuity and, therefore, although they could run like the wind, they simply were not managerial material. That was *it*, as the saying continues to be. Al was out of baseball like *that*! The news of his conclusions about the black race was carried throughout the land with the same intensity and solemnity as would another attack on Pearl Harbor.

"We are so relentlessly mindless. Reporters like to picture themselves as independent thinkers. In truth, with the exception of 13-year-old girls, there is no social subspecies more slavish to fashion, more terrified of originality or more devoted to group think."

Michael Kelly
The Washington Post

XV

WHAT'S NOT REPORTED AND WHY?

Now and then we hear complaints from either the left or right, depending on whose ox is being gored, that *The Media* do not report news that would prove or disprove a point.

Now that John Kennedy's sexual activity in and out of the White House swimming pool is well documented, many of those televised media panels deal with the question of why this activity was not reported. The answer from experienced journalists old enough to have covered Washington in the early 1960s is usually, "We simply didn't know," or "That kind of stuff was not reported in those days." The latter answer begs the question: "Why not?" The press mentioned Thomas Jefferson's alleged sexual activity with one of his slaves. Grover Cleveland's paternity was reported and used as campaign fodder against him. So why wasn't Franklin Roosevelt's relationship with Lucy Mercer reported or Lyndon Johnson's rather hyperactive libido material for a tabloid news story?

A broad consensus lays the blame for the current reporting of anything sexual involving any politician at the feet of Gary Hart, who made the mistake of inviting reporters to follow him around to discover any extra-marital activity. They did and the rest is history.

When John Dean faced imprisonment because of his Watergate activity, a story was bandied about that he feared going to prison because of what he'd heard that seasoned inmates are said to do to attractive young males. Fortunately for Dean, he served his time in a federal detention center, far removed from any maximum security facility. That was in the early 1970s, over 20 years ago. Based on sporadic reports of prison guards who force female inmates to have sex and guards who allow female or male inmates to violate fellow inmates, it seems that this heinous practice continues unabated in prisons today. Could a diligent press put an end to what is apparently a long established practice? If it couldn't stop it, it probably could help to minimize the practice. Virtually any Hollywood film dealing with prison life, makes sodomy and rape an integral facet of prison life for many.

Harvard law professor, Alan Dershowitz, has frequently mentioned that police routinely lie when testifying before a jury, even though they take an oath to tell the whole truth and nothing but. This charge has been made off and on over the years. Apparently it continues unabated. So…why isn't this reported by intrepid reporters on the police beats of the nation? (Dershowitz is on so many talk shows that he should be listed in *TV Guide* as a regularly scheduled program.)

President Clinton got himself in further legal trouble when he testified before a federal grand jury. He was asked why he had testified earlier that he did not have sexual relations with Monica Lewinski. This was of special interest because his attorney, Robert Bennett, told a judge that his client did not have sex with her in no way at all, no how. The president replied that he wasn't listening when Bennett made that comment, although he sat cheek by jowl with Bennett. A video of his testimony before the judge in the Paula Jones civil suit against him clearly showed that the President was, in fact, paying close attention to what Bennett told the judge. The video was unsealed along with other testimony in the Jones case and available to any network to show. It wasn't shown until the Republican majority counsel showed it during his presentation at the Judiciary Committee hearings. Various members hinted that the video would prove the President's prevarication, but it was almost impossible to learn this from a watchdog media.

The Clinton-Lewinski scandal brought before the public as never before the term, "Spin." Almost nightly, commentators mentioned "White House spinners," as in, "The White House has put an opposite spin on today's testimony," and so on. Occasionally someone mentioned that "Spinners" appearing on talk shows were given talking points by someone in the White House. Never was a report given that identified exactly who in the White House gave all of those Spinners their talking points each day. This, by definition, would have made a juicy news story.

There seems to be an indifference among reporters to get at the heart of various stories which is in violation of the old standby of journalism: Who, what, when, where and (importantly) why. For instance:

Harriet Higsby sues Corporation XYZ because the brassier she bought cut off circulation and caused her grievous pain. Her attorney is shown on television commenting on his client's case. Never is it reported just how the attorney landed the case. Is he an ambulance chaser working on a 40-60 percentage contingency deal? Did he call the woman or did she call him?

.When a White House "Spinner" shows up on Larry King's show, why doesn't Larry ask whether the guest's remarks were discussed by him or her in the White House and, perhaps, rehearsed beforehand? Maybe he doesn't want to know.

Every now and then someone changes the journalistic landscape. Bill O'Reilly hosts "The O'Reilly Factor" on FOX News Channel. He was a "reporter" for years on a local New York station before hitting it VERY big on FOX. He rants and raves five nights a week on a variety of subjects. Some time ago he began asking how much money Jesse Jackson makes. Almost nightly he kept up a drum beat: "Where's the IRS in all this?" he would ask. "Where did all that money come from to pay his mistress?" he continued. Night after night. Not an uninteresting series of questions, questions never before asked by any other journalist. After awhile stories in print and on the air surfaced, somewhat timidly, pursued the story that O'Reilly broke. His relentless "reporting" forced other media to ask hitherto untouchable questions of the "Right Reverend." It does seem strange why certain subjects remain hands-off, subjects that, almost by definition, cry out to be covered.

XVI

KEEPING TEDDY VIABLE

A strong case can be made that the main reason Teddy Kennedy is still in the U.S. Senate is that the news media have handled him with fleece gloves and have given him a free pass to linger on Capitol Hill as long as he wishes. Moreover, a case can be made that he should have resigned from the Senate after the Chappaquiddick tragedy for allegedly breaking several laws, but he got off with a rap on the knuckles. Today, there are pundits who describe him as being one of the all-time great U.S. senators, right up there with Henry Clay. One suspects however, that the Kennedy "machine" has more than a little to do with this public relations effort.

It's all part of a pattern that began with the tragedy of Jack Kennedy's assassination on November 22, 1963. It set off a series of events in this country that are still being felt today. For the first time in history it came to pass that the Presidency was considered by many the private domain of a single family.

Kennedy's widow, Jacqueline, began almost immediately to establish an aura about the deceased leader, an aura that would translate his personal taste in music and "Camelot" in particular, to identify his abbreviated administration with the court and round table of King Arthur. Both legends were myths.

It has been widely reported that Bobby Kennedy actually tried to bar the new President from entering the oval office soon after the assassination. It is reported that he told Johnson that he had no right to enter the office. Thus began a Presidency in exile. After a period of mourning, Bobby Kennedy began a program to educate himself, mature, and attract as many loyal supporters as possible to make his ascension to the White House almost a foregone conclusion sometime in the future. Kennedy loyalists rallied round and left no doubt that they were all for a return of a Kennedy to the White House.

Kennedy decided to establish a political base from which to operate. He blatantly challenged an incumbent U.S. Senator, Kenneth Keating, for the Democratic nomination. It meant little to Kennedy or his supporters that Keating had a solid reputation as an effective legislator and was, unlike Kennedy, a bona fide New Yorker. Kennedy won and spent a brief time giving Lyndon Johnson fits from his minority Senate seat.

In time, Kennedy made the inevitable run for the Democratic presidential nomination, but ran into strong opposition from Senator Eugene McCarthy, of Minnesota. McCarthy managed to give Kennedy strong opposition, especially by derailing the Kennedy juggernaut in Oregon. He narrowly lost the California primary, a Kennedy victory that was nullified by an assassin's bullet in a hotel kitchen. The ugly Democratic convention in Chicago followed, but a little noted event took place as the politicians gathered to decide who would be their standard bearer against Richard Nixon in the general election. There was a boomlet for Teddy Kennedy to receive the party's call although he was still young and still relatively immature. But a boomlet there was nonetheless. There remained a strong body of opinion, almost solely among Kennedy loyalists, that a Kennedy must someday return to the White House. If it had to be immature Teddy, so be it.

Once Nixon completed his reincarnation and back from the ashes portrayal of a determined Phoenix, he ran headlong into the Kennedy legend and the Kennedy drive to regain control of 1600 Pennsylvania Avenue. Then came Chappaquiddick. Various reports have concluded that Teddy Kennedy almost certainly violated several laws as he extricated himself from the tragedy and embarrassment of the death of Mary Jo Koepecne. He made his famous nationwide television address after having consulted with an array of Kennedy loyalists— many of whom were lawyers, officers of the court and all that. He got the networks to cover his *mea culpa* remarks although he said he was speaking to his constituency, the voters of Massachusetts. He was considered at a dead end as a far as presidential ambitions were concerned. But, then, Jimmy Carter defeated Gerald Ford and was to become a one-term president. As Carter attempted to win renomination for another chance to represent his party, this time against Ronald Reagan, Kennedy suddenly entered the fray. He claimed that many Democrats approached him and urged him to run against Carter in the primaries. Carter, they said, was far too weak to win again. So Kennedy went across the country more or less telling voters that, well, Carter was too weak to be the party's standard bearer.

Roger Mudd of CBS interviewed Kennedy on national television and asked the question heard round the country, a question that would put an end to Kennedy's campaign against Carter. Mudd asked Kennedy why he wanted to be president. Kennedy's reply was garbled, disjointed, vague and totally inept. The reaction was immediate and fatal. Kennedy ended his attempt to gain the nomination. He later showed his disdain for Carter—for anyone other than a Kennedy who would dare to want to be president, by ignoring him on the convention platform. He gave a tremendously effective speech at that convention, replete with sounds and effects associated with his brothers. It was his last attempt at anything other than retention of his Senate seat.

Until Chappaquiddick and even after, it was the media that kept Kennedy afloat politically. If Kennedy wanted to succeed his brother,

Jack, and carry on the memory of Bobby, even though common opinion was that he was far from being their intellectual equals, the media enabled him to do so. They truly did what they could to keep the Camelot flame lit throughout the land. There is an enormous body of evidence that many in the media, especially those who had been close to Bobby, did what they could for "The Family."

When Teddy made his run against Carter, sitting behind him on every platform was his doting wife, Joan. They had been estranged for some time, but he was running for the *big cohuna* now and there she was, dutifully smiling and looking on lovingly. A family man all the way! The media undoubtedly knew about their marital difficulties but were loath to report about it. Better to simply show her in her support mode and hope that, someday, life on the political beat would come alive with the possibility that a Kennedy would return to the White House to demonstrate how Presidential duties could be carried out with class.

Once Teddy dropped his ambitions to replace Carter, he and Joan went back to their pre-campaign status. During the campaign, Teddy reportedly tricked Joan into meeting him for a loving lunch at a chic Manhattan eatery. She said she showed up somewhat excited by the invitation to, perhaps, résumé their marriage. Teddy showed up as did a host of photographers to record their togetherness. The photographers did their work and left as did Teddy. Joan said that her husband hardly spoke to her. She had been set up for a Photo-Op to help his chances. The media reported none of this. It seems understandable that the media keeps hands off a married politician who is a philanderer. However, when a couple live apart and obviously are about to say "Sayonara" to each other, isn't it reasonable that a reporter tells the public that the candidate whose estranged wife sits on a platform, smiling to beat the band, is actually trying to pull a fast one?

The effort by the media to keep Teddy (or any Kennedy) afloat belies the usual litany that reporters cover the news without fear or favor. But how does this square with the media's non-coverage of Eugene McCarthy giving a serious speech and the deluge of coverage of Bobby Kennedy giving essentially the same speech? This was a complaint a frustrated McCarthy often made to reporters. This clearly illustrates that much of the media sees its duty as reporting the news maker and not necessarily the news.

Probably the most damning indictment of media partisanship is the coverage of Jack Kennedy in the House, Senate and on the campaign trail to win the 1959 Democratic presidential nomination. Besides reporting (reporters) and opining (columnists), members of the Washington Press Corps spend much of their non-reportorial time gossiping about who's doing what to whom, etc. There is not much that goes on in Washington that one of them doesn't know and eventually fills in everyone else who still doesn't know. We now know that Jack Kennedy was extraordinarily active as a seducer of women, truly priapic. Much has been made in revisionist biographical works of how he essentially stood up Jackie before and during their marriage to enjoy himself with the *femmes du jour*. It has even been reported that he had to be talked into returning to the U.S. from a European sexual junket to be with Jackie who had just lost a baby.

The point of this is that on today's omnipresent panels manned by seasoned journalists who were around during the Kennedy era, to a man or woman, they claim they knew nothing about Jack Kennedy's sexcapades. This strains credulity, to say the very least. Even the *Washington Post*'s Ben Bradlee of Watergate fame has often claimed that he knew nothing about Kennedy's philandering. Jack Kennedy was not exactly secretive about his extra-marital activity. Bradlee's sister was said to be a long-time lover of Kennedy. Bradlee and his wife were very close personal friends of Jack and Jackie.

As Henry Thoreau said, "Sometimes the circumstantial evidence is very strong, as when then is a trout in the milk."

It is easy to develop a "Devil Theory" of the Kennedys. If one of them gets into trouble someone, somewhere will surface quickly to explain how dedicated that Kennedy is to all manner of humanitarian enterprises. Teddy has been the target of many disparaging remarks about his lack of intelligence. One of the most apt was when his opponent for the Senate said that, "If his name were Smith, it would be a joke."

It is always "The Family." When Kennedy was granted a seat on the Senate Armed Services Committee, one more than is allowed, the reply from Democrats was something like, "Oh, he's a Kennedy." A Harvard law professor reportedly said of his first campaign in 1962 that Teddy had a so-so academic record, he had virtually no professional or business background and that his candidacy was, in effect, absurd and an insult to one's intelligence. As mentioned earlier, as recently as late 1999, the drum beat had begun to position Teddy as a truly great U. S. senator. Not just an outstanding senator, mind you, but, by implication, worthy of a state funeral once he passes from the scene. It is mysterious how the media gave the Kennedys a pass into the national pantheon, but, somehow, didn't do the same for the Rockefeller, Forbes, Bush or other families that had lots of money and great track records of outstanding performance in various fields of endeavor.

"You see, we live in an age where the line between 'news' and 'fluff' is blurrier than ever."

Steven Brill
Brill's Content

XVII

WITHOUT FEAR OR FAVOR

It has become axiomatic that a newspaper or television network, when it makes a *boo boo* and gets a story wrong on page one or at the opening of a news show or a *News Break*, will never give a correction or retraction the same play as the original story. "They had it totally wrong," the offended party usually says, "but when they admitted they were wrong, they played it on page 56 and you could just barely see it."

This situation has been played out countless times over the years. Someone being interviewed claims to be misquoted, but the story runs and lots of attention is paid. But when the story is found to have been inaccurate, the news medium that got it wrong is slow to shout "Mea culpa!" Now that the world has come to know and love the phrase "he said, she said," from the Clinton-Lewinski scandal it is easy to understand the reluctance of any medium to admit that it got a story wrong. Nowadays many reporters go into an interview with a tape recorder. The interviewee is asked whether he or she minds having the interview recorded. If he or she says "You bet your ass I mind," the reporter must resort to note taking or rely on memory of what is said and jot down notes once out of the room. If a recorder is used and a dispute arises about what an interviewee actually told the reporter, the tape can be played and the reporter (hopefully) can prove that what appeared in print or what was said during a telecast actually was said. But often, a recorder is not used and an interviewee claims that the reporter got it all wrong and asks that the newspaper or TV station apologize and/or produce a retraction. Imagine the reporter in question entering his or her boss's office. The interview actually wasn't anything world shaking and if the complaint hadn't been made, no one would have cared a whit about who said what. But the complaint was lodged and questions must be asked. The reporter claims every word in the story was spoken by the subject.

"But she says she never told you she had five abortions before she won the Miss America contest," the editor says.

"Charlie, I stand by the story, word for word."

Who will ever know who is telling the truth? This example is of a bona fide journalist doing his job. If most of the bizarre stories that appear in the *Star* and *National Inquirer* go uncontested, what do we think the chances are of a hapless interviewee calling a lawyer?

(Although, based on what we have learned from watching the O.J. trial and the nightly analysis of the Clinton scandals, there's always the chance that some lawyer will call the interviewee and suggest, perhaps, that a case can be made. No money up front, mind you, payment only if a financial settlement is made.)

Much of what the public watches deals with politics in the national arena. Sam and Cokie, Wolf Blitzer, Chris Matthews, Larry King (Larry King??!!) C-Span, Jim Lehrer on PBS, Tim Russert and the other political commentators talk endlessly about what is going on in Washington. Most journalists in the country have little or nothing to do with this. Most work for small media enterprises, either print or broadcast, and tune into the *celebrities* mentioned above just like the rest of us. While Wolf is covering the White House for CNN, Harry Blow is covering the construction of an asphalt plant on what used to be farm land. Again, even at the national level, there is usually not much real news to report. This is why mistakes are often made in getting facts straight. Let's say the reporter has a rather mundane job as described earlier. He or she has a "Beat" that has nothing to do with sports, local politics or any of what would be considered the juiciest assignments. Suddenly, there is an explosion at one of the asphalt plants. People are killed. There is danger to the entire community unless a massive evacuation takes place NOW! For probably the first time since the hapless reporter has been working for the paper or station, there is *news* to report. The reporter will get to use all of that classroom and on-the-job training he has accumulated for years. Details will have to be gathered story leads written and, probably interviews taken of asphalt plant officials and family members of those killed. This is what the journalist lives for, not unlike the soldier who hates war, but loves to be sent into battle where someone can be shot or stabbed or blown up. For as long as the asphalt explosion story plays out, there will be endless reporting and little sleep. If Lady Luck is cooperative, the reporter might even wind up with one of those awards that are always being distributed to journalists who are lucky enough to cover a story resembling news. Many factual errors will be contained in the many stories filed, but no one will really notice or care. There was excitement for a change and a chance to apply reporting techniques long dormant.

XVIII

THE BEST AND BRIGHTEST

If a journalist makes a handsome income a natural assumption is that that person can be trusted. After all, he or she is near the top of the income chain, is educated and well spoken. Respect must be paid. Salaries in the millions are television generated. A top print columnist or editor can pull down a comfortable $250,000 or so. Remember, too, that the $1 million-plus TV star probably earns as much as the print counterpart makes in a year by giving speeches to corporations eager to spend big bucks to entertain and impress the troops at sales meetings and the like by having a TV star entertain them for an hour or so.

The point is that the best of the best don't cheat the audience they address. They are, by definition, straight shooters. If this be true, how do we account for the following examples of downright deceitfulness?

. ABC has attracted a lion's share of the Sunday morning viewing audience of politically minded citizens ever since David Brinkley gathered George Will and Sam Donaldson under his wing to give a solid overview of things political. Cokie Roberts joined the team later on. Brinkley retired and ABC gave the show to Sam and Cokie. George Will remains as the program's deep thinker. Later, former White House spin master, George Stephanopoulos, and *The Weekly Standard*'s William Kristol joined the program as the resident Liberal and Conservative, respectively.

Each Sunday they have various political celebrities appear who field questions from this team of inquisitors. It's the same each time. Sam asks embarrassing questions, George jumps in with penetrating questions and Cokie smiles and adds analysis borne of years of being a child of politics. (She's the daughter of the late Congressman, Hale Boggs.) George and Bill jump in later when they're invited to join the others. The show runs an hour, from 11:30 until 12:30. At about 12.22 Sam or Cokie graciously dismiss George and Bill and George. They then tell us to stick around because just the two of them will "be back." Viewers do as they are told and watch the umpteenth commercial shown during that hour. True to their word, they come back to sum up the prior dynamite erudition. Wrong. Sad to say that when they return as promised, they return to spend a few seconds promoting various ABC programming that is scheduled for later that day or later that week.

When Cokie tells us she and Sam will be back, the implication is clearly to put a ribbon around what the public has been watching. Instead, they become hucksters for the network and cease to be prestigious opinions makers. They cannot be proud of this duty, although at a few million a year one supposes there isn't much they would not do if ABC told them to do it.

* * *

Let's say that the Dean of the Washington Press Corps is, by definition, an honorable person, fair minded and, without question, ethical. Historically, this person has probably been in demand to give speeches to college students and other groups anxious to hear from the horse's mouth how journalism is practiced at the highest level. There is great collegiality among this honored "Dean" and his brethren in the field of journalism.

Rewind to November 22, 1963 on a street in Dallas, Texas. Merriman Smith, the aforementioned Dean at that time, was in the first press pool car behind the main presidential motorcade. Shots were heard; all hell broke loose. An agreement was in place that called for Smith, the senior Associated Press correspondent, to have first dibs on the telephone in the car. (This was, of course, long before every other citizen owned a cellular telephone.) The agreement stated that should something of interest occur, Smith would have a reasonable period during which to call in his story to the A.P. He was to then relinquish the phone to the United Press correspondent so the U.P. could put the story on its wire. But, who in the hell could have guessed that the news that day would be an assassination attempt on the president? What happened in that press car that fateful day reminds one of that great line in *Dr. Strangelove* when actor Peter Sellers as the president scolds irate scuffling generals by telling them that, "There will be no fighting in the war room!"

Smith could not, would not give up the phone. The obviously maniacal U.P. representative began pummeling Smith while the latter continued to add details to his unfolding story. Two grown men at the top of their prestigious profession cracked under pressure and became examples of how not to behave while covering a major news story.

* * *

Peter Arnett probably wishes he'd never heard of CNN. He became embroiled in a CNN imbroglio that involved a report that the U.S. military used nerve gas to kill off deserters during the Vietnam war. CNN later backed off the story, firing the reporter and producer responsible for its content. Arnett almost lost his job as a result. Overnight his reputation as a dynamic war correspondent, earned in Vietnam, Desert Storm and elsewhere, began to crack at the seams. What the public learned from the incident was a little known practice by highly regarded TV news stars of going on camera, mouthing words written by someone else. This is understandable when deadline pressure is considered. What got Arnett in trouble (and all media stars by implication) was that the impression given was that he was the author of the words he spoke. Either he was a genuine reporter who writes his own stuff or he's one of those empty suits, a talking head. It didn't take long before Arnett and CNN parted company for good.

Suggestion, just for the fun of it: The next time Jennings, Rather, Brokaw or any of the other mega-buck TV talking heads appear at a corporate sales meeting and the highly paid guest speaker offers to answer a few questions (for $50,000 you would think that's the least he or she can do) the following should be asked:

"Sir (Ma'am) how long does it take you to write the script that you deliver each night on your news program?" The answer to this question should be worth a barrel of laughs.

XIX

RANDOM THOUGHTS

Historically, tabloid newspapers have gotten a bum rap from full sized newspapers and other dispensers of news. Tabloids simply know what appeals to the *hoi polloi*. Forget the focus groups that say readers want international news, national news, how-to features, sports, etc., in roughly that order. Tabloids know this is malarkey. They know more of their readers prefer racing results and the funnies to knowing who is doing what to whom in Bosnia. They know it is axiomatic that there is no high brow in the lowbrow, but there is a considerable amount of low bow in the highbrow.

If it is winter in states where winter means cold weather, local television stations go gaga over the low temperatures. If the weather happens to be reasonably cold, but not unbearable so, TV talking heads throw in the wind-chill factor to kick their weather report up a notch.

"Well now, it's thirty degrees at the airport, but when you factor in that wind that's picking up outside, you're looking at a brutal twenty degrees out there. So bundle up and don't go out if you don't have to."

Sound familiar?

* * *

Some years ago the National Football League was on strike and there was no Sunday or Monday football to keep American men away from books and conversation with family members. This being America, the networks who were without games to televise and make money from did the obvious next best thing. They began televising Canadian football games! The usual network broadcast teams sprang into action and gave the games the same play-by-play excitement and hype as they would do for the NFL. There was no difference. The sportscasters used the exact phrases and indulged in the same hokey small talk that has become part of their shtick. The obvious assumption is that they would have done the same had the networks opted to televise bull fights to fill the void.

"Oh, wow, Pat, did you see El Mundo pull off that unbelievable *midi veronica*? He's really moving with great intensity. It's obvious that he's come to play…and that's no bull. Ha Ha Ha."

The only conclusion to be reached is that the networks assume (correctly) that the American public will buy into anything they put on the air. This is, alas, almost certainly true.

John Randolph Parker

XX

HOW RUPERT MURDOCH SAVED THE DAILY NEWS

Those of us who were there consider what happened akin to Doug Flutie's famous "Hail Mary" touchdown pass when Boston College broke the heart of Miami University. It's a good example of what goes on behind the walls of major opinion molders who don't hesitate to shine the glare of truth into any and all areas of public concern, but draw the line at coming clean when they are the target.

In the very early 1980s the nation's largest daily newspaper, *The New York Daily News*, was hemorrhaging money Its parent, Chicago's The Tribune Company, grew tired of losing money at an alarming rate. Advertisers were deserting the *News* mainly because it had the smell of a newspaper whose days were numbered. One of the primary reasons for this impression was a hatchet job performed almost daily by Rupert Murdoch's *New York Post*. Murdoch's paper was losing enough money, itself, to make the *News* look downright prosperous. Murdoch was determined to kill off his rival on 42nd Street and have the lucrative New York tabloid world to himself. The News had always been a cash cow, pouring millions into the coffers of The Tribune Company. In one of life's great ironies, Murdoch, a transplanted Australian, kept reminding New Yorkers that the *News* was owned by a foreign government in Chicago. The *News* had been such a strong presence in New York that it had kept several other tabloids from closing for many years. The News was so rich in advertising that it couldn't accept it all. What advertising it couldn't squeeze into its chock full pages, it directed to the *Mirror* and other tabloids who could use the money.

Alas, times had changed. Every day but Sunday (years later the *Post* began publishing a Sunday paper) Murdoch's paper hammered the News via house ads that screamed in huge headlines that the *News* was a dinosaur that had seen its better days. It was out of touch and couldn't touch the *Post* for relating to the needs of New Yorkers. After all, the *News* was owned by an outfit in Chicago, the Second City, for crying out loud. In short, according to the *Post*'s reasoning, the *News* had lost its usefulness to New York and the *Post* was ready and willing to fill that need.

Murdoch's campaign worked. *News* employees became frightened for their future employment. One of the sales managers said that his mother called one day after reading one of the *Post*'s house ads and asked, "Are you all right, son?"

Interestingly, key reporters and editors who thought nothing of bringing down local, state and federal politicians were among the most frightened. Daily, they would ask those involved on the business side to level with them about the paper's future. Morale was at an all-time low.

Then it happened. Robert Hunt, sent by the Tribune Company to be president of the *News* to stop the hemorrhaging, called a top secret meeting in an conference room on a upper floor of the famous art deco building. Sales managers, top brass, and the paper's ad agency assembled to hear what Hunt had to say. He explained that the paper's *mole* at the *Post* reported that Murdoch was about to launch a circulation building promotion called "Wingo." He said that Murdoch used the promotion with great success in Sydney, Australia and in London.

"We're going to beat that turkey at his own game," Hunt said passionately. "He's going with a top prize of $25,000 and will launch "Wingo" in three weeks. We're going to give $50,000 and launch ours in two weeks. We're going to call ours "Zingo.""

The result was an all-out promotional war. Murdoch was forced to double his top prize money. The move energized News employees almost magically. Almost broke, the News, under Hunt's bold leadership, decided to give away $50,000 each week, plus money for secondary cash prizes. The "Hail Mary" pass was caught and the

News beat the *Post* at its own game. The *Post* continued to treat the *News* as if it had leprosy, but the *News*, while no longer the nation's largest paper, is still the tabloid favorite among New Yorkers.

Oh...Probably the main reason why the *News* did not die when it was supposed to is the following give and take, according to what executives were told at the time: The Tribune Company had been told that it would cost about $80 million to close up shop in New York. On the day it was slated to happen, The Tribune Company reversed itself. It was told at the eleventh hour that, oops, the cost to close the paper would be a prohibitive $125 million!

A revealing sidebar to all this is that *Daily News* executives literally chased television reporters and camerapersons from the art deco building when they showed up to learn the latest in what was going down at the nation's largest circulation newspaper. The paper that would think nothing of getting details for a news story by just about any means could not abide inspection of itself by others.

XXI

A REVIEW OF THE REVIEW

By definition, PBS lends credibility to any presentation on television, at least by today's shaky standards. After all, it's PBS!Gather together a few "journalists," give them an hour or so to exchange political news and views and you have a program of the highest possible quality. None of that crazy hyped up stuff you see on the *McLaughlin Group*, *Cross Fire* and other show biz news entries.

Let's take a close look at this weekly program, *Washington Week in Review*. After all, it must attract a fair share of viewers interested in who is doing what to whom in the White House, the Pentagon, Capitol Hill, Foggy Bottom and other inside-the-beltway venues. First, a moderator is retained who is above reproach such as Ken Bode, Dean of Northwestern University's School of Journalism. He keeps the show moving along at a reasonable clip. Next an assortment of serious journalists are assigned seats around a table—a couple females, a couple males, each with some sort of expertise in a specific area, such as the Pentagon, White House, Capitol Hill, Foggy Bottom...you get the picture.

A subtitle for the program could be "Once Or Twice Around the Table." The moderator kicks off the show by making some sort of general statement about current political events. Then he says something like, "Harry, the Air Force said this week that it wants all pilots to wear kilts. Tell us, just what's going on across the river at the Pentagon.

Harry dutifully begins to explain why the Air Force wants its pilots to cross dress, all the while referring to notes as he gives the nation the inside story on this vital question. Although he has just been asked the question, he is armed with notes with which to give his inside scoop. The moderator's original question was posed as if it were something that just occurred to him as a topic that might be of interest to the viewing audience. The fact that the Pentagon expert has notes from which to make his or her reply clearly indicates that the program isn't quite what it is billed to be. What, then, is it? Why, it's SHOW BIZ!

Anyone who has watched this show for any length of time will agree that after several years on the air, seldom has one of these experts come through with any fresh insight. Without fail, the overview presented on any given program is merely a distillation of what the "expert" and any well-read viewer has read or heard about a given subject in recent days.

The program showed it's true colors in 1999 by unceremoniously unloading Ken Bode, a *very* long- term host on the show, in favor of a youngish female. The explanation? Management wanted to give the show a little more juice, a little more pizazz. This happened not at FOX or CNN or CBS or NBC or ABC. It happened at PBS!

XXII

SOUND BYTE WARFARE

Chevy Chase said he was and we were not. The same can be said about the hoards of journalists who show up on television *news shows*. They are being watched and we are not. They enjoy the spotlight and the rest of us tune in to watch them. It makes little difference that these commentators are constantly ridiculed as being less than meets the eye. After all, they landed the spot on television and pull down healthy supplemental incomes while other wannabes beat down doors to join them.

Now that there is a proliferation of cable channels to compete with the Big Three-plus-Fox there is a resemblance to major league sports. Expansion has diluted quality. So-so infielders earn salaries that would make most corporate CEOs rage with envy. So it is with broadcasting. The media—radio and television, that gave us Murrow, Sevareid and Cronkite have spawned a plethora of talking heads that seem to have appeared from out of nowhere.

The criticism beat goes on, but new *news* programs pop up in *TV Guide* with predictable frequency. To paraphrase Frank Sinatra, "Criticism, there's been a lot," much of it justified. Via a full-page ad in a recent *New York Times Magazine, Salon.com ("*makes you think*")* told the world of Sunday *Times* readers that:

"Tonight on Pundit TV" there would be "pay-by-the-hour windbags, moralists for hire and other assorted dispensers of reddi-whipped political wisdom."

It is difficult to find fault with the copy message that followed: It reported that journalism, politics and entertainment have begun to merge. Because of this, *pundits* have increasingly become performers. They posture and declaim—that's what performers do and that's what they do. The ad concluded, "As long as political commentators, like sports - radio jocks, are hired on the basis of who has the loudest, most obnoxiously nasal voice, we'll be forced to endure their sermons. And as long as those commentators remain drawn from a stagnate, inbred pool those sermons will be inane."

After reading the ad and agreeing with every word the following observations can be made:

Cross Fire: CNN's nightly answer to professional wrestling. Otherwise serious journalists such as columnist Robert Novak and a host of other members of the National Press Club "argue" left and right and close with a smile after 22 minutes of posturing liberally and conservatively. Pat Buchanan is usually on the right when he's not on a leave of absence to run for President. Many people watch this show religiously even though it is blatantly SHOW BIZ.

Hannity & Combes: Sean Hannity and Alan Combes talk as fast as a speeding bullet, non-stop, from the right and left. They have many guests with whom they take turns disagreeing. They are both erudite and definitely at opposite ends of the political spectrum. But they are, truth be told, performers whose job it is to squeeze 44 minutes of entertainment into their allotted hour.

This Week with Cokie and Sam: It began under the glare of David Brinkley's star and has lost any semblance of credibility since he departed to appear in commercials. Now, the American public is treated to political insights delivered by arch conservative Bill Kristol and George Stephanopolos, the former Clinton Spinmeister who once bashed an anti-Clinton book, written by an FBI agent with 30 years of service. George showed up on every talk show listed in TV Guide to tell the world that the author was, "without any credibility."

The McLaughlin Group: Pure entertainment with otherwise bona fide journalists doing their best to behave badly. Thought leaders presumably watch this!

The Beltway Boys: This show on Fox News made it official: Journalists will do anything as long as they can appear on television. Morton Kondrake and Fred Barnes, veteran McLaughlin Group loudmouths, are basically serious political writers who will perform anywhere it seems, when the red light goes on.

It is interesting to note that *The New York Times* and *CNN* turned down subsequent advertising by *Salon.com.* They claimed the Internet news journal was a *competitor.* Suffice it to say that the *Salon.com* advertising campaign was hard hitting and made light of mainstream media's stance as serious news providers.

XXIII

FLASHES IN THE PAN

Boredom. That explains what has happened to journalism in recent years. A journalist's career has become that of ennui, except for the rare occasion when a president is caught getting it on with a young intern or when the nation goes to war or when there is an assassination attempt. Generally, there isn't much news to report so boredom is the lot of the news reporter, unless, of course, he or she can land a spot on one of those televised news programs which can mean more money and more public recognition. Jack Germond, curmudgeony columnist for the *Baltimore Sun* has explained it this way: "You could write your fingers off for 25 years and never get the kind of hearing you could get from shooting off your mouth on television for half an hour every week." Germond is a former regular on the *McLaughlin Group* and has been on a weekly Washington, D.C. station's news panel for years.

One of the big reasons why print journalists risk extinction in the face of television's dominance is that the public is bored as well. People old enough to remember the first moon shot understandably were excited as hell when Neil Armstrong stepped onto lunar firma. But how many people tune in to watch today's shuttle launches and landings?

The networks have already begun to give national political conventions diminished air time. They have become old hat. The public is finally on to the phoniness and manufactured excitement among the delegates, some of whom are ritually caught napping as the speeches drone on. The public has been conditioned to tune out conventions. With the aid of remote channel changers, they switch to a sit-com or ball game whenever what is being televised from the convention floor becomes *deja vu* all over again.

Since Larry Bird, Magic Johnson and Michael Jordan demonstrated how basketball should be played, the current crop of wannabes go through the motions but fewer people are watching. ABC's *This Week with Cokie and Sam* has become predictable and its ratings have slid downward since David Brinkley left the show.

There are simply too many options. Evenings from 8:00 to 9:00 give us CNBC's Chris Matthews's *Hard Ball,* and Fox News's *The O'Reilly Factor.* After that, Geraldo Rivera weighs in for CNBC. He has since moved to FOX News to cover wars. *Hannity and Combes* follow O'Reilly to keep the political news ball rolling. Surfers also can stop by *Larry King Live* to see if he has any guest worth watching for a few minutes. These programs occasionally are interesting to watch, but during the Monica Lewinski *Year from Hell*, these programs were watched with enthusiasm because sides were taken by viewers who were either pro or anti-Clinton.

The diminution of respect for journalists (right down there with used car salesmen) seems to validate the adage, "Familiarity breeds contempt." Murrow, et al. were, by comparison, still behind the Wizard's screen. Ed, we hardly knew ye. These days, Sam Donaldson, Cokie Roberts, Geraldo and the gang are celebrities right up there with Harrison Ford and Barbra Streisand. They are seen together at Washington outings such as "Roasts" and the like. The public has long noted that most reporters are at least as well dressed as the highly paid personages they cover. This is so because the reporters are often much better paid than the reportees. Today it is reasonable to assume that every newspaper journalist worth his or her byline is in frequent touch with their local or network TV stations, volunteering to go on camera at a moment's notice, hoping against hope to be, well, noticed.

XXIV

PLAGIARISM ON THE MARCH

It is getting so that otherwise astute editors no longer can tell the difference between plagiarism and, well, plagiarism. Every day at newspapers and television stations throughout the land, journalists re-write stories written by others that have appeared in or on a competitor's outlet. Radio news broadcasters have always read their material from off a wire service. In a pinch they read directly from that day's newspaper. Don't forget that *Daily News* editor mentioned elsewhere who screamed, "Hey, without us, you bastards wouldn't have anything to report!"

Many years ago a media observer speculated that the secret to *Time* and *Newsweek* was reading and rewriting the contents of "The Week in Review" section of the Sunday *New York Times*. There is more than a germ of truth in that comment. Journalists begin their day by reading a newspaper or, more likely, several newspapers. They probably watch a TV news program as they dress for work. Often, an editor will hand a reporter a news clipping from another paper and say something like, "Find out what you can about this and give me about 15 column inches on it." The reporter then makes a few calls and asks questions based upon what he or she has read and eventually fleshes out another reporter's handiwork and it becomes his or her own. This has been called *recycling of words.*

Enter Bill Barnicle, a much-honored and very popular *Boston Globe* columnist for over 20 years. He was highly respected throughout the journalism world, enough so that he was named godfather to a child of NBC's Washington Bureau Chief, Tim Russert. Barnicle made a media splash when he was fired by the *Globe* for passing off some of comedian George Carlin's material as his own. There was such a hue and cry from fellow journalists and faithful readers that the *Globe* relented and welcomed him back into the fold.

Enter a former editor of the *Reader's Digest* with a long memory. He recalled a piece Barnicle submitted to him years before. The editor said he rejected the work because he detected plagiarized portions. He promptly FAXed this information to the *Globe* and Barnicle was out the door for good. A la Bill Clinton's guru, Dick Morris, who rose from the ashes of an embarrassing incident involving a prostitute,

Barnicle was soon snapped up by a Boston television station to do commentary.

A lady at the *Washington Post* was an up and coming star writer. She wrote a feature about drug use by a youngster who was going nowhere fast in Washington, D.C. The story was so descriptive and moving that Janet Cooke brought Pulitzer Prize honors to herself and the *Post*. Later, it was found that Ms. Cooke was so enterprising that the boy she described and the tale she told about him were actually fiction, made up by her to impress her employer and as it turned out, the Pulitzer judges. She was fired. Unlike Barnicle, she has had difficulty landing a cushy spot with any medium.

More recently, a red hot writer for the *New Republic* was shown the door because it was learned that many of the outstanding stories he turned in to earn his 25 year-old "Whiz Kid" reputation were fabricated by him. Names, places, entire stories were works of his feverish imagination. He was prolific enough to also contribute pieces to *Rolling Stone*, *Harper's* and *George*.

Another instance of a columnist lifting material written by others and passing it off as his own involved the *Indianapolis Star and News*. The ousted columnist was reported to have said of his dismissal over what he called, "a handful of stories," that it was "unfortunate…considering that I wrote 5,200 stories during the 12 years I worked for the Star."

It has become almost trite to mention that the media gives huge headlines or lots of drum rolls to front-page stories that prove to be inaccurate and that the subsequent "apology" usually winds up far inside the paper or dealt with swiftly on air.

The story of the ill-gained Pulitzer gained public notice, but quickly faded from the national consciousness. On the seemingly omnipresent media panel shows that crop up on cable channels, one or more of the panelists usually says something like, "It's up to us to police ourselves." Such sentiments have been uttered for decades with no discernible change in how the media handle *boo boos* or otherwise fail to do what is right.

Howard Kurtz, the *Washington's Post*'s media observer, seems to have missed an important point when he wrote in his column: "Journalist Sydney Schanberg argued...that the Press doesn't cover the press and has gone soft on itself. But Schanberg misses a recent explosion of media criticism—on Web sites like *Slate* and *Salon.com,* in magazines such as *Steven Brill's Content* and in alternative newspapers that nip at the heels of big city dailies." The problem that Kurtz failed to understand is that it takes outsiders to call attention to the errant ways of the mainstream media. (Even though they say they are determined to police themselves.) A real "whopper" was a Baltimore Sun music critic who was fired because a reader whistled on him for including copy from an opera album jacket in his review.

XXV

THE BABES TAKE OVER

Heaven only knows what Helen Thomas, dean of the Washington Press Corps, must have thought when she spotted a *TV Guide* cover story, "How Women Took Over the News."

Ms. Thomas always looks as if she has just come in from a Nor'easter, besmudged with typewriter ribbon ink, perhaps a No. 2 pencil stuck rakishly in her hair. By contrast, NBC Today's co-star, Katie Couric smiled out at America on the cover, every hair in place and perfectly made up. The article began this way: "With captivating interviews and compelling insight, Katie Couric and Barbara Walters and other top female journalists are bringing us the stories that matter and the scoops that score—and creating a powerful connection with viewers."

Ms. Couric made a comment that inadvertently spells the difference between the old days and the present. "I have a lot of male friends in the business," she said, "who are extraordinarily talented, but there is something about a maternal comforting presence that is helpful to people at a time like this. (A child had been killed.) We cover things with a more feminine touch, a female sensibility…Call it a journalism of empathy…it's a sense of compassion mixed with *chutzpah*."

Imagine, if you will, PBS's Jim Lehrer during his famous interview with Bill Clinton when the Monica Lewinski story broke, taking Bill's hand and saying something like, "There, there, Mister President, it's going to be all right."

The *TV Guide* article reported that ABC, for example, nearly doubled its number of women correspondents from 1991 to 1998. It might be noted that this is the same period of time that Bill Clinton took center stage and captured the hearts of American women. Most if not all the ladies mentioned in the article seemed to have a common bond: They were hired for their looks and ability to read from a Teleprompter. Later, they would do interviews and make a name for themselves as *journalists*. Diane Sawyer rose through the journalistic ranks as an operative in the Nixon White House and went with the disgraced president to San Clemente to deal with his dimly lit future. She later parlayed a dazzling attractiveness and landed with a Louisville, Ky. television station. She admitted in the article that she got the job the old fashioned way, "Pointy bras…we're talking twin peaks and hair spray."

One can imagine Ken Bode, dean of Northwestern's outstanding School of Journalism encouraging his faculty to make certain not to omit the Twin Peaks maneuver from their lectures. Bode was summarily replaced as moderator of PBS's *Washington Week in Review* by 37 year-old Gwen Ifill, a former NBC correspondent who has covered Capitol Hill. Ms. Ifill has the distinction of having been a print journalist with the *New York Times.* (This means that besides being able to give an on-camera report without stuttering she, by definition, can WRITE! She actually can tell many of the other feminine television reporters what it is like to cover a story without a cameraperson or producer anywhere to be found.)

A female editor of a very popular women's magazine actually said on a talk show that she liked Bill Clinton and would vote for him a third time because, she said excitedly, "He's sexy!" If she had been around, Lincoln and Harry Truman wouldn't have stood a chance.

XXVI

THE LACK OF POWER OF THE PRESS

Let's examine for awhile the incident that will be remembered as *The Bill and Monica Affair.* From Day One, Clinton was justifiably pilloried in the media as being less than morally clean. He was bashed daily in the press and on the air. Sam Donaldson proved himself to be a flawed prognosticator by declaring immediately after the news broke that the Clintons would be out of the White House within a few days. Chris Matthews did his darndest on CNBC's *Hard Ball* show to shame Bubba out of office, but, well, Bubba was still there to the bitter end. Bill O'Reilly at Fox News pummeled Clinton relentlessly, but he was still there. *New York Times* columnists Maureen Dowd and William Safire weighed in throughout that period with less than laudatory pieces. Ms Dowd made fun of the President and occasionally, the First Lady, but never really came out and called him a cheat, felon and/or pervert. At one point Safire called Ms Clinton a "cogenital liar." These powerful pundits, writing for the most powerful newspaper in the nation failed to direct public opinion to demand resignation or influence legislators who knew that a guilty conclusion to impeachment was apparently the only alternative to urge him to leave.

One of the few winners was the ever-popular Geraldo Rivera on CNBC. Geraldo followed Matthews's *Hard Ball* show with a defiant defense of Clinton. In the face of mounting circumstantial evidence that Clinton was lying his way out of his predicament the way that Nixon never could. Geraldo shamelessly defended him, frequently quoting "my sources close to the President," to make his nightly rebuttal to Matthews and others. Geraldo stood alone against the onslaught of Rush Limbaugh, The *New York Times* and several cable network heavy hitters and wound up on the winning side. Go figure. (As mentioned, Rivera has joined Fox News.)

Imagine the allies bombing Dresden for countless hours and, lo and behold, Dresden remained as pristine as ever. Not even a scratch. That will be the legacy of William Jefferson Clinton. If Ronald Reagan was Mr. Teflon, Clinton was Mr. Teflon with an extra coat of WD-40.

A classic scene in movies that pits a good guy against a bad hombre and a good laugh is the aim is when the good guy gives the huge ogre his best punch and the bad guy doesn't flinch. The good guy's expression says it all. It's time to get the hell out of there. The *Washington Post's* Sally Quinn must have had the same feeling when she did a critical feature on Bill Clinton. Everybody who was anybody was talking about her demolition job on Clinton. It had no discernible effect on Clinton's approval rating. Her piece told the world that the elite upper crust within the Washington, D.C. beltway hated the Clintons. She reported that those on the inside of D.C.'s power elite tended to consider the Clintons, well, not very classy and, therefore, not worthy of their 1600 Pennsylvania Avenue address, not to mention use of Air Force One. Ms. Quinn's effort came and went with little or no effect on the viability of the First Family.

XXVII

THERE IS NO THERE THERE

I once asked a colleague who was born and raised in New York why Joe DiMaggio was named the best center fielder in the 20th century when many people thought otherwise. "Probably because he played in New York," was his immediate reply.

And so it goes. In the United States of America, the ol "Melting Pot," big cities in big states seem to count and small towns in small states get short shrift. If the New York Yankees are in the World Series the media ballyhoos the prospect of an exciting slug fest. Let the Seattle Mariners go against another expansion team and the media predict a "snoozer," a really dull, not-worth-watching non-event.

Same with the Super Bowl. Give the public the Cowboys against the Packers, but avoid at all costs New England against Tennessee.

(Question: Why are there so many teams in the first place if many of them are deemed worthless? Could it possibly have something to do with money!?) Same with politics. Mentioned elsewhere in this study was the Oregon primary that pitted Bobby Kennedy against Eugene McCarthy. McCarthy pulled a decisive upset. The media chanted "So what, on to California where real people live." The media actually denigrated Oregonians for being relatively well mannered and affluent and mostly white. The state came in for criticism because it didn't have enough ghettos.

One can depend on the media to winnow out what they consider non-persons with absolutely no chance to make a successful run at the presidency. Newspaper columnist and sometime co-moderator of CNN's *Cross Fire*, Pat Buchanan, has usually been given fairly positive coverage because he makes good copy and knows most TV anchors who are likely to invite him to appear on their shows during the primary season. Gary Bauer, a mild, clean cut Casper Milquetoast of a man by comparison, was hardly noticed by the media. The same with razor sharp but too independent, Alan Keyes. Keyes is black and could be the first black president, but there is no way the media will take him seriously and, therefore, he can run but that, as they say, is it.

Bob Dole best summed up the media's tendency to play favorites, based on their being good copy. Given a chance to chat with a few reporters during the 1999 primary season, he noted, "Hillary Clinton is running for the Senate and her every move and comment are covered like a blanket. My wife is running for President and it's hard to find any coverage of her campaign at all."

That distaff curmudgeon, Camille Paglia, put it this way in one of her columns:

"...My confidence in (Elizabeth) Dole's political instincts and potential was never high, but I must say the media had incredible gall to complain about Dole's withdrawal when they didn't do squat to help her—so besotted were they with the chimera of Hillary Clinton's possible senatorial run in New York...The lack of serious press scrutiny deprived Dole of the opportunity to learn from her mistakes and to make key adjustments of her saccharine delivery and often nebulous policy statements."

XXVIII

C-SPAN FOREVER!

It was many and many a year ago that a man named Brian Lamb put together a cable channel, hired a few well mannered and bright on-air folk and slowly but surely became what every other television network would like to be. There doesn't seem to be much if any Teleprompter reading. Everyone of Lamb's team looks as though he or she could be a college professor or high school principal or simply someone you'd really like to get to know. They are to a man or woman, soft spoken, polite, attractive and refreshingly, it seems, honest.

Unlike the C-Span wannabes at the network and local news stations, the C-Span hosts and hostesses seem to be without egos. On any network or local news program a viewer will hear the name of the person seen on camera ad nauseam. Remember how it's done at the beginning of each "show." "Hi there, I am Hilda Higsby...and I'm Freddy Smiley..." At the close of the show, it's "This is Hilda Higsby"..."and this is Freddy Smiley saying good night. See you tomorrow!"

You don't hear any names during a C-Span telecast. During the morning programming that usually has the network host read interesting political news from various newspapers no name is mentioned. Later when experts, usually with differing political leanings, are welcomed aboard, the names of the guests are given but the name of the host or hostess remains a mystery. In this age of giant-size media egos, one finds this policy of anonymity as refreshing as a cold air bath. C-Span is as close as one gets in this country to the laid-back, intelligent approach to presenting news.

C-Span's primary mission is to televise the goings on in Congress each day. What else it does is make a mockery of what the commercial networks (and even PBS) do by comparison. One hears constantly from the public that more and more people tune into C-Span during political conventions or state-of-the-union addresses and the like because the viewer isn't saturated with constant commentary by on-air experts who talk incessantly about what is being shown. "I get so tired of hearing them go on and on instead of just allowing me to listen for myself," is the battle cry heard more and more as the years pass by.

Brian Lamb obviously sees no need for drum rolls at the beginning of each segment of C-Span's day. His strange, albeit refreshing, approach to television has resulted in his name being mentioned on air once (sic) during the more than two decades C-Span has shown the others how to do it right. Unlike Jennings, et al., Lamb and his merry band of hosts and hostesses, C-Span's lineup seems to be devoid of any fashion plate aspirations. They are well dressed; that's about it. The C-Span crew add new meaning to the phrase, soft spoken. Unlike the network "stars" who always have a measure of phony urgency in their voice, Lamb and his team speak softly and carry a big dose of believability.

Competitive pressures being what they are, even C-Span is responding to the challenge of a number of imitators. The cable channel now has an Internet web page. Occasionally during a morning program, the host will talk with an on-camera web page specialist. Movement seems to be the answer to all news programs who make changes they think they must make to keep an audience. Don't forget Jennings, Brokaw and Rather walking around their sets like chickens with their heads cut off.

AND THEN CAME THE INTERNET

Times have changed so much in recent years that it is difficult to tell where the news begins and where it ends. There are still newspapers, news magazines, and news programs on television. But with the introduction of the Internet, all bets seem to be off. Microsoft's Bill Gates has even gone so far as predicting that the Internet means the eventual disappearance from the scene of, BOOKS!

Herewith an example of the Internet merry-go-round. Michael Kinsley is a Harvard Law School graduate who, somehow, has made it big in all facets of the news business. He was an editor and columnist for The New Republic. William F. Buckley apparently fell in love with him and had Kinsley host various debates Buckley arranged to have on Public Television. (This, in spite of the fact that Kinsley, a la Anthony Hopkins's portrayal of Hannible Lector in Silence of the Lambs, never blinks.) Moreover Kinsley would have an occasional op-ed piece in various major newspapers. He even showed up as a regular residing Liberal on CNN's Cross Fire, a program that is nothing more than out and out show biz.

Then, there was a news bulletin that Kinsley was giving up Washington political commentating and joining Bill Gates in Seattle, Washington as editor of Gates's new Internet "newspaper", SLATE. A fair amount of money had to be involved to have Kinsley move to Seattle! But he was given the opportunity to be in charge of a brand new news vehicle and that challenge (plus the money) must have been too enticing to turn down. SLATE took off and one assumes more people than Kinsley and his staff read its daily output. Eventually, Kinsley began showing up on occasional television news programs and, as predictable as still another sunrise, he became a columnist for the Washington Post. The Post exposure did just that: It enabled Kinsley's writing and thinking to be seen once again, not on a screen, but on paper, on paper that appeared in Washington, D.C. He retained his position as editor of SLATE, but, like the Terminator, he was BACK!

XXIX

EXIT LAUGHING

An earlier chapter described how television news "teams" exaggerate non-news items they pass off to the public as news. Just as this opus was about to go to press, *The New Yorker* came through with a ringing endorsement of that conclusion. The venerable (or at least it used to be considered as such) magazine uses its last page to make a point about whatever is on its mind that week.

What caught our attention was a headline that read: **The Alarmist News Network: Worst-Case Scenarios—Around the clock!**

In six cartoonish panels the following points were made, not too far removed from actual news broadcasts that come our way throughout each day.

1) The female anchor reported that President Bush slipped in the shower that morning and almost fell. Her male counterpart, then, sent viewers to "TV Doctor Bob" who was to discuss the "brush with disaster."

2) Dr. Bob explained that thousands of Americans are seriously hurt each year in bathroom accidents and, based on that, it was entirely possible that Bush could have fallen, struck his head on the tile, and wound up in a coma, from which he might never recover.

After that enlightening news, they turned to the weather.

1) The female allows as how it is sunny and warm on the East Coast at present, but that doesn't mean there couldn't be a category 5 hurricane later that summer and entire cities could be destroyed.

2) The male anchor opines that it is probably a good idea to stock up on canned goods just to be on the safe side. The gal then concludes that even then there is a risk of botulism and other contaminants. Her partner then asks whether the West Nile virus will "kill us all". He promises to explore that possibility right after "these messages."

The point is that *The New Yorker's* parody was based upon a generally held opinion by most people that there really isn't much real news out there.

This is all a reminder that the cat is out of the bag, so to speak. The other day the news reader for one of the cable network news shows, told viewers that *The National Inquirer* had a story that was to appear the next day that would add something of significance to the then breaking story of Congressman Gary Condit (D., CA). This reminder of an upcoming story wasn't about something the *New York Times* was going to carry, but the anti-Christ of publications. Not long before that everyone in a major (legitimate) news medium condemned anyone who lent credence to the "Tabloids" which, obviously, had no credibility at all. Now, they were calling the world's attention to a "breaking story" in one of the hated weeklies. No more was there mention of double sourcing to pin down accuracy. By the beginning of the 21st century, it seemed to be every publication for itself and see what the guys in the back room will have.

XXX

THE HORSE'S MOUTH AS GOOD SOURCE

This might be a stretch, but let's try it on for size. This report has indicated that there is little there there in the television news business. Some of it was opinion, some has been spoken truth. Therefore, we'd like to close with the verity that was explained by not an onlooker, but someone who is in the field every day, going where few men dare to go to bring Americans the news as he sees it and who collects a whopper of a paycheck from one of the beloved networks.

NBC's National Correspondent Bob Faw seems to be an honest enough journalist who probably has seen one too many Jessica Savichs cross his path on the way to pick up expense account funds. Faw recently spoke at one of this nation's colleges. He was to receive a fairly hefty honorarium for showing up. To his credit he turned his honorarium back to the college to be included in a special fund that was earmarked for a memorial fund for a famous journalist. Because of his position with NBC, there was a large turnout to hear what he would have to say. People are attracted to "celebrities." Following is a portion of what he had to say about the field that mentions Edward R. Murrow at every opportunity.

"In my business virtually everything is for sale. It is a different universe than the one I so naively entered some 30 years ago. The news business has changed and so have we. Back then, we were more or less in the business of delivering the news. Now we're in the business of delivering audiences. Back then, the line between news and entertainment was clear-cut. It was church and state. Now those lines are hopelessly blurred. If the truth be told, we spend far more time in the television news on how an interview looks than on what it says."

We should keep Faw's words in mind the next time we sit down to watch the news to keep ourselves well informed. After all, the drumbeat and frantic music at the beginning of the program indicates that what we are about to see and hear is of the utmost importance. This is NEWS!

THIS IS CNN?

As this is written, CNN, the cable all-news network that brought the world the Gulf War and went to the head of the news class as a result, was in deep doo doo. The proliferation of cable networks and the emphasis on around-the-clock news finally caught up with the brain child of Ted Turner. Bill O'Reilly, the curmudgeony talk show host on Fox News Channel passed Larry King as the most watched show of its genre. (Bear in mind that Rush Limbaugh keeps reminding his vast world that few people watch the cable news shows. He estimates that under one million folk watch King and far fewer tune into the others.)

As a result of the viewer slippage at CNN, there has been a plethora of changes at the top, middle and bottom. Administrators who helped put CNN on top of the heap have been dismissed. On-air talking heads have been guillotined into unemployment and new faces adorn programs that have been around for many,. many moons.

"Everything has been changed except the name," is one headline America has been clobbered with as CNN attempts to change its image to meet the competition.

"We've changed because you have changed," is another one, if you can believe that. One asks: Would any of this *toro merde* have come America's way if CNN had not slipped in the ratings? Of course not.

So new music precedes many of the programs that have been around for a long, long time. The music, one assumes, is an important change in what CNN is offering. A new face saying the same thing is another big change. New graphics, new music, new faces, it all adds up to more of the same only with new packaging.

Packaging, that's what it's all about. We have returned to Dan Rather's sweater.

Oh well.

LAST THOUGHTS

Not long before the final chapter of this book was written, a group of crazed terrorists changed our world, probably forever. Once again, broadcast and print journalists sprang into action and gave us all the news we craved to receive. It is entirely possible that by the time this publishing process is completed much of what has been described will have changed. For instance, Geraldo Rivera actually went to Fox News Channel and asked to be hired to cover the war in Afganistan. Greta Van Susteren, now has her own late evening program on Fox, having been hired away from CNN to handle late night duties in the never ending cable news wars, although several critics can't imagine why. As mentioned, she has gone from practicing attorney to television personality. THIS JUST IN! Just before moving over to Fox Greta, 47, had surgery to remove bags under her eyes. Enron Corporation has made other companies (and their accounting firms)

143

run for cover. Will any of that corporation's officers go to jail? We will find out. But keep in mind that the savings and loan scandal of a few years ago was of enormous size and implications and it wasn't long before it was business as usual.

Sportscasters are as daffy as ever. Watch any pre-game show and you will be witness to grown men and women acting childishly. There is little or no hope that this trend will ever change.

Repetition is the culprit that is bringing down the quality of the news media. One simply cannot view tragedies too many times before becoming somewhat indifferent. Times have changed, drastically. Not too many years ago the United States was a simple society. We had one of each: Burl Ives was the nation's folk singer; Eddy Arnold was our country singer; Fred Waring led the nation's choral group; Kate Smith was the official singer of *God Bless America;* Bing Crosby made Christmas special by singing *White Christmas,* long before political correctness reared its head. There was one boxing champion for each weight class and baseball players stayed with the same team for longer than a fortnight. Allegiance was pledged to the nation's flag and the word, God, was pronounced in public on many occasions. Journalists smoked cigarettes with abandon and many drank liquor on the job. There were a handful of automobiles for sale and a few soft drinks available. Cigarettes gave off a smell of tobacco instead of a chemical cocktail. More than a few citizens lived into their seventies and beyond without giving a chocolate nut sundae a second thought. With few exceptions, the only persons who wore tennis shoes did so when playing tennis. Proliferation of talent and interest in all categories of life has changed the social landscape forever, so much so that it is all one can do to listen to many renderings of the national anthem before sports events. And, well, so on.

There have been hints that Dan Rather might say Sayonara to network television in the near future and some even talk openly about possible successors to Tom (Marbles) Brokaw. The Today Show's Katie Couric has renewed her contract for an amount of money that puts her in the same class as the Sultan of Brunei.

Plagiarism has reared its ugly head once again. Stephen Ambrose, of all people, has been caught with his prose unattributed to another writer who had the idea first. As if that wasn't enough, the hitherto untouchable Doris Kearns Goodwin followed suit by being caught for doing the same thing. Ambrose apologized for his mistake. It has been reported that Ms. Goodwin paid out a sizable amount of money to the writer from whom she borrowed to show her contrition.

The end is not in sight. Most cities have but one major newspaper. As mentioned, Don Hewitt of "60 Minutes" has predicted that the three major networks just might forget about evening news programs because local stations beat them to the punch during the day.

Times, they are a changin' to beat the band. It has been some time since we lost Murrow and Sevareid, Huntley and so many other familiar faces. We must prepare ourselves for the retirements of Rather, Brokaw and Jennings. We can certainly do it. We have done it so many times before.

ABOUT THE AUTHOR

John Randolph Parker spent 10 years as a member of the Washington Press Corps, covering the Pentagon and both houses of Congress. He later became Advertising Director of 50 Plus Magazine. This is his fifth book: NO BUTTS ABOUT IT: How to Want to Stop Smoking, was his first, followed by "Burp": A Journal About Food and How to Enjoy It; How to Sink A Sub: A Substitute Teacher's Rather Strange Appraisal of the American Educational System; and most recently, The Kennedys Are Driving Him Crazy! He and his wife, Marcy, operate The Parker House, a Bed & Breakfast in Chestertown, MD. For the past three years he has entertained residents of Kent County and beyond via his weekly radio program, "For the Love of Food" heard on WCTR, a local station in Kent County on Maryland's Eastern Shore.